Critical Thinking and "r"eligious Folklore

Reader and Workbook

By David Garnett

Every effort has been made to secure the required permission for the selections in . I respectfully request that any copyright holder/s whose permission does not appear here, please contact me at the following e-mails: grinite1@lycos.com or villa45@operamail.com. so that I can make the necessary arrangements and adjustments. Please use copyright and the title of this book in your subject line.

If you are interested in hard bound copies of this book, contact the author at the emails above. Please write folklore and the title of the book in your subject line

PRINTED IN THE UNITED STATES OF AMERICA

PREFACE

The aim of *CriticalTthinking and "r"eligious Folklore – Reader and Workbook* is to help students think critically about and analyze different kinds of writing. They can then arrive at their own understanding about the meaning of a reading selection. Students learn how to organize their thoughts and analysis so that they can write about their understandng of each reading selection.

Critical Thinking and "r"eligious Folklore - Reader and Workbook is a book of literature selections from "r"eligious folklore (See **What is this book about?** In **COURSE INTRODUCTION** which follows **Table of Contents** for a discussion of *"r"eligious folklore*.) The workbook is self-contained. All the readings are included in the workbook. Students complete most of the comprehension exercises and short written assignments in the workbook too.

Critical Thinking and "r"eligious Folklore - Read and Workbook is designed for students in or above the middle school level. If you review the selections, you can easily see which can be used with lower level students, e.g., the stories St. George and the dragon in the chapter called **Dragons**, and which, with upper level students, the selections in the chapter entitled **What the divine has touched**.

Students use folklore, such as short stories, poetry and ballads, lives of holy folk, etc., as the foundation for analyzing and thinking about the content, meaning, and themes of a selection. Graphics thinking organizers are the main vehicle that students use to help themselves:

- analyze the meaning of each selection they read;
- organize their thoughts in preparation for writing.

The organizers cover such thinking or analytical areas as: comparison and contrast, classification, sorting, cause and effect, sequencing, etc. There is extensive guidance on how to fill out a graphic thinking organizer when each is first introduced. After applying an organizer to a particular text, students write their analysis, based on the reading selection and their completed thinking organizer. The section of the book entitled **COURSE INTRODUCTION** gives details about the relationship among reading, meaning and writing.

The analysis using the graphics thinking organizers in *Critical Thinking and "r"eligious Folklore - Read and Workbook* as well as the preparation exercises for writing can be completed individually or in a group. A companion volume *"Snipp snapp snute, så er eventyret ute" – Folklore Reader and Critical Thinking Workbook* has additional critical thinking materials and different reading selections.

Students who use the volume should have more options for analyzing and writing about other texts and literary selections they meet. They will probably be able to transfer much of the critical thinking "techniques" used in *Critical Thinking and "r"eligious Folklore - Read and Workbook* to other curriculum areas in their school work.

To Elvira and John
for all their patience

Critical Thinking and "r"eligious Folklore:
Reader and Workbook

Table of Contents

Table of Contents, Continued

Table of Contents, Continued

Table of Contents, Continued

Table of Contents, Continued

Table of Contents, Continued

Table of Contents, Continued

COURSE INTRODUCTION

What's this book about?

"r"eligious traditions?

This book is about religion – religion with a small "r." "r"eligion focuses on traditions of various faiths. These are stories, folktales, folk hymns and songs, sayings, etc.

Some of these "r"eligious tales and stories have been handed down by word of mouth, orally, from one person to another. Eventually, they were written down.

The selections in this volume are not Religious, with a capital "R." They are not usually found in the holy books of any faith such as the *Holy Bible.* The *Qu'ran (Koran),* and the Hebrew *Pentateuch* or *Torah.* You might call these "r"eligious traditions a kind of religious folklore.

- Parishioners and worshipers are often the primary source for these works.

- These tales were probably carried in the everyday conversation of lay folk, who usually came to a house of worship, such as a church, a mosque, a temple, etc.

- Grandmothers and grandfathers might have told them to their grandchildren, who, when they became grandparents, told the same stories to their grandchildren.

- Sometimes, authors wrote a "r"eligious writing to expand on a religious theme or explain an original holy verse or work

---

A Word about Usage

In this book, the phrase ***the divine*** refers to the name for the one God in most religions today for example, Yahweh or Jehovah in Judaism, God or the Lord in Christianity, and Allah in Islam.

What's this book about?, Continued

WHAT A CHAPTER LOOKS LIKE

Chapter Part	Description
Intro. and Overview	<ul><li>Lists and explains the texts of the chapter.</li><li>Discusses the objectives of the chapter.</li><li>Includes special information pertinent to the chapter.</li></ul>
Text(s)	<ul><li>May introduce the author(s) of the text(s) in the chapter.</li><li>Presents the selections for you to read.</li></ul>Includes follow-up exercise(s) to help you understand the content of the text(s).
Thinking Organizer	<ul><li>Presents the thinking organizer(s) that you will use to analyze the text(s).</li><li>Explains how you will use the thinking organizer(s) with the text(s) of the chapter.</li></ul>
Writing	Here you: write about the results of your completed thinking organizer or develop a special project. This section includes guidance on either the written work or the project.

Continued on next page

Reading, Meaning and Writing: Important to you, the reader

Reading

Besides reading various selections, you may also learn about the genre or type of literature you study in a lesson. This may include the life of the author, who wrote the text selection(s).

In presenting the selection,

- New or difficult words and expressions are explained. In some instances, you have to look up the words and then do a vocabulary exercise to show you understand the words.
- You also get hints or tips on what to look for as you read.
- To help with the content of the text, you do mini-exercises. These study tables help you to think more carefully about what you have read.

Meaning

Meaning in a text is not always so easy to grasp. Meaning is a two-pronged effort.

First, as your read,

- You are trying to arrive at what the author wants to say. You have to deal with what is clearly and directly stated by an author.
- You also have to deal with what is underneath, not directly stated – this is called implied meaning. You will learn more about this in some of the lessons.

Working with a text helps you to:

- Form you own understanding of the author's thoughts.
- Deal with how the selection affects you personally.

Continued on next page

Reading, Meaning and Writing: Important to you, the reader, Continued

Writing

Writing connects or ties together the texts and their meaning to you. You express you thoughts

on the meaning(s) in the texts,

and

how important the meaning is to you.

You will write about you own involvement with the texts in this student workbook.

Thinking Organizers: Focus of Your Reading

Definition

The learning focus in the chapters of *Critical Thinking and "r"eligious Folklore* is the thinking organizer (which has been around for many years). A thinking organizer is a pictorial or graphic format that helps you, the reader, to

➤ Figure out and analyze texts.

➤ Organize your thoughts about the text in preparation for writing.

Figuring out

In other words, a thinking organizer helps you to figure out the following:

- What the author means.
- How the writer gets across the main points to the reader.
- How the piece of literature is designed or put together.
- Why the work is important, particularly to you.

Continued on next page

Thinking Organizers: Focus of Your Reading, Continued

Thinking Organizer like a Map

A thinking organizer is like a map.

- On a map, you can see the specific city or town where you are going.
- You can also see the larger area around the town at the same time.

A map shows a general broad structure of an area as well as a specific smaller or mini-area. Organizers help you in the same way.

- You can see the specific point in the text that you are writing about.
- At the same time, you can also keep in mind the whole text.

An example of a thinking organizer is shown below with guidance on how to use it. Look at the organizer and read the guidance that follows it.

Cause(s)

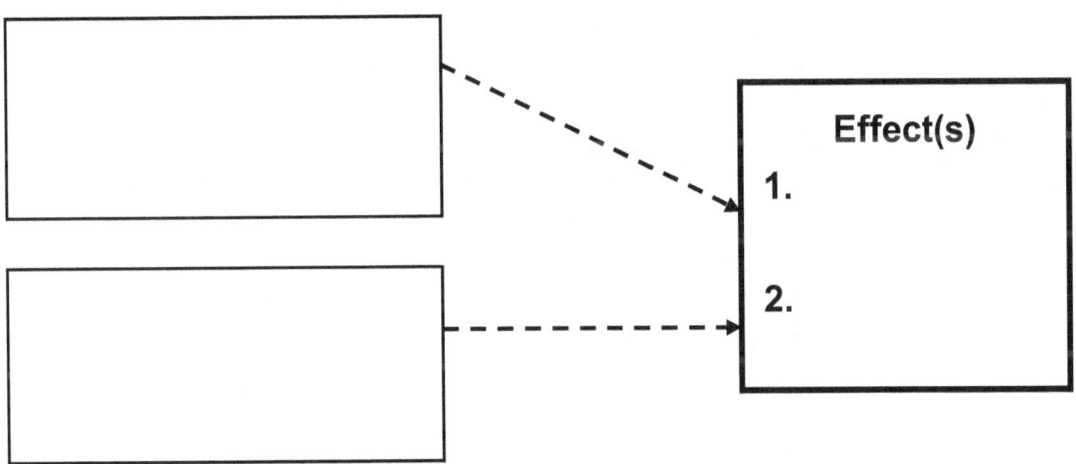

NOTE: Instructions for this organizer follow on the next page. You will need to look back at this organizer as you read the guidance for it.

Continued on next page

Thinking Organizers: Focus of Your Reading, Continued

Directions for the Organizer on the Previous Page

Cause(s)

Along the left side of the thinking organizer is a vertical row of **Cause(s)** blocks.

> **Here you would fill a cause in each block.**

Effect(s)

On the right side of the organizer is a block labeled **Effect(s)**.

> **Here you write the effect(s), one beside each number.**

Filling in the organizer

On the **CAUSE AND EFFECT** thinking organizer,

> Fill in the blocks.

> Use only the material from the paragraph that you have read to fill in the blocks of the organizer.

(Although there is no text to go with this table, it is not difficult to see what you would need to do when you have one.)

Writing

With your completed thinking organizer and the original text, you would write a short paragraph on the causes and effects of the subject in the thinking organizer.

You would need to support your statement about causes and effects with examples from the reading selection and from your thinking organizer.

Chapter I
Houses of Worship

Introduction and Overview

Introduction

Everyone who worships needs a place to pray. You know these places by many names: In Judaism the place of worship is called the synagogue, in Christianity, for most, a church or a cathedral; and in Islam, a mosque (*cami'i*).

In this chapter, you will read about various places of worship. In some cases, you will discuss these places by comparing and contrasting them. Others you will classify.

What to do:
Lesson
Objectives

You will:

➢ Use some important thinking organizers to analyze the selections about places or houses of worship.

➢ Learn how to use various study tables that are part of this book.

➢ Use thinking organizers to help you write about the different houses of worship.

Companion
Guide

This workbook is a companion to *"Snipp snapp snute, så er eventyret ute" – Folklore Reader and Critical Thinking Workbook*, which has additional critical thinking materials and different reading selections.

Continued on next page

Introduction and Overview, Continued

Lesson Components

A text or group of texts that you will read. Most of the writing and other work you do require you to read and refer to these text resource(s).

Any of a number of activities or exercises which you need to complete. These activities may include:

- Vocabulary exercises.
- Questions to answer.
- Study tables to complete.
- Thinking organizers (graphics or picture diagrams) to fill out.
- Written work to plan, organize, and write.

All these activities should help you to read and understand the texts or to write about them.

You may have to complete a project, which requires limited research.

Lesson Content

The selections that you will read, think about, and write about in this chapter are descriptions of the following:

- St. Eufemia Church.
- Suleymaniya Mosque.
- A Roman-Saxon cathedral in England.
- A village mosque.

Let's get started

The first worship place you will read about is an ancient Christian church that was located in Turkey, across from Constantinople, which is now called Istanbul.

As you read, pay attention to all the different things the author describes in his writing: the setting, the size, number of buildings, use of the buildings, etc. These are what you will write about later in this chapter.

Church of St. Euphemia

The church of St. Euphemia the Martyr, is situated in the district of Chalcedon in Bithynia, ... [a short distance from the Bosporus]. The site is a beautiful spot, of so gentle an ascent [slope], that those who are on their way to the church, are not aware of their immediate approach, but suddenly find themselves within the sanctuary [church] on elevated ground. Extending their gaze from a commanding position, they can survey the level surface of the plain spread out beneath them, green, waving with corn, and |beautiful with every kind of tree. ... Directly opposite is Constantinople [present day Istanbul, Turkey] ... Thus ... the beauty of the [church] site is enhanced [increased] by the view of so vast a city.

The Church of St. Euphemia consists of three immense buildings. One is open to the sky, including a [large] court, which is embellished [decorated] on all sides with columns. Next to this building is another, nearly resembling it in its length, breadth, and columns, [Only this second building has a roof] ... .

On the north side of this second building, facing east, is a round building, [beautifully capped by a dome. [Inside this domed building are] ... columns of uniform materials and size. These columns support a gallery under the ... roof, so ... that the faithful may ... [pray] and be present at the service. ...

Towards the eastern part of the domed building is a splendid enclosure, where the bones and relics of the saint are preserved ... in a long coffin ... . There is an aperture [opening] in the left side of the coffin, secured with small doors, through which the bishop and priests introduce a sponge attached to an iron rod to reach the saint's sacred relics. ... After turning [the rod] a round, they draw it out, covered with stains and clots of blood. On witnessing this, all the people bend in reverence.

Adapted from: Evagrius Scholasticus, *Ecclesiastical History* (AD431-594), translated by E. Walford (1846). Book 2: Chapter III. Not in copyright. www.ccel.org/ccel/pearse/morefathers/files/evagrius_2_book2.htm.

Continued on next page

Church of St. Euphemia, Continued

Mini-exercise

➤ Reread the selection; then, do the study table below.
➤ Check **all** boxes that apply to the description of the church.

	The Church of Euphemia was located in Constantinople.
	There was no difference between the first and second building of the church.
	The bones and relics were located in the second building.
	The third building was triangular in shape and had a hole in its roof.
	People prayed primarily in the domed building.
	The saint's bones were preserved in a coffin.
	This description emphasizes the gardens surrounding the church.
	The description is mainly about the structure of the church.

Sketch the buildings of St. Euphemia

These buildings are typical of a church in the time of St. Euphemia. The description of St. Euphemia Church is easy to understand. You could almost draw the church with its buildings. Try it and see if you can.

On the next page sketch out the three buildings, how they would appear if you were looking from a helicopter above them. We have put some directions on the map to help you orient your drawing.

- "**N**" stands for north.
- "**S**" stands fro south.
- "**E**" stands for east.
- "**W**" stands for west.

Your drawing doesn't have to be full of details. **You just want to show the three buildings and how they are arranged.**

Sketch St. Euphemia Church

N

W   E

S

_____

An Islamic Mosque: Suleymaniya

A Complex of Buildings   Islamic mosques also have a definite structure. Let's take a look at one. Then you will work out the design of a mosque complex.

"The Mystical Dimensions of Suleymaniya Mosque In Istanbul"
Semih Ceyhan

Sinan, the architect of the Suleymaniya Mosque, boasted to Suleyman:

"My Emperor, I have built you a mosque that will remain on the face of the earth until the Day of Judgment, and when [the angel of death] *comes to shake Mount Damavand from its foundations, he will be able to shatter the mountain, but not this dome."*

from Evliya Celebi

The Suleymaniya complex, sponsored by Sultan Suleyman the Lawgiver [was] built by Mimar [architect] Sinan (c.1491-1588) in Istanbul between 1550 and 1557. Suleymaniya is the largest of the Ottoman buildings … . It consists of … the monumental Suleymaniya mosque and two mausoleums (tombs of the sultan and his wife Haseki Hurrem Sultan, built in a walled enclosure) at the center, separated by an outer courtyard from four general madras's [schools].

[There are also madras's of school and learning centers as part of the Suleymaniya most.]The madras's consist of two specialized madras's-one for the study of medicine, and the other for the study of hadith [the says and life of Muhammad] and a Koran school for children. There are also a hospital, a hostel, a public kitchen, a hamam [public bath], a caravanserai [lodgings for travelers], and rows of small shops.

Suleymaniya Mosque is the main building in this complex. … A spacious courtyard surrounds the mosque. There is another inner courtyard surrounded by porticos with 28 domes supported by 24 columns. This inner courtyard is a little smaller than the main building. In the middle is located a sadirvan. In the four corners of the inner courtyard stand four minarets having a total of ten balconies.

Before you continue reading, select the best answer to the question:

There were about _____ buildings in the Suleymaniya Mosque complex.

    a.   2-4   b. 6-8   c. 10-14   d. 16-20

Continued on next page

An Islamic Mosque: Suleymaniya, Continued

The acoustics [the way sound travels], … one of the distinctive features of the building, were achieved by placing 64 pots in different places in the walls and the floor. … the stained glass [windows are] … not original. When the mosque was built there were 4,000 oil candles, the smoke from which could have endangered the paintings on the walls. The architect avoided this [problem] by creating a system for the circulating … air inside the building.

Adapted from: http://www.rumi.org.uk/event/handout/suleymaniya.htm

---

Mini-exercise   Do the study tables below. Follow the directions for each table.

One problem that Sinan the architect avoided was _____

(Circle **all** letters that apply.)

a.	breaking the stain glass windows.
b.	bad breath from all the people who assembled in the hall.
c.	the problem with leaking water from the roof.
d.	the damage that smoke from the candles could do.

The basic plan for the complex is _____

(Circle **the** letter that applies.)

a.	one main worship center with two tombs and additional buildings like madras's.
b.	three main buildings with surrounding shops.
c.	a large gallery for visitors and a worship center.
d.	a place for men and women to worship; a separate place for children.

Continued on next page

An Islamic Mosque, Continued

There are _____ around the main building

(Circle **the** letter that applies.)

a.	three fountains.
b.	two pools with fish.
c.	two courtyards.
d.	two playgrounds for children.

Comparison and Contrast: Definitions

Purpose

You are going to compare and contrast the two places of worship, St. Euphemia Church and the Suleymaniya Mosque.

IMPORTANT: Axis/Trait

Before you begin, you need to understand the definitions of compare and contrast.

In doing a comparison and a contrast, you have to look at something that is common to both items you are comparing and contrasting, for example in the case of two stories:

- Settings of the two folk tales.
- Descriptions of the characters.
- How the characters behave.

You can probably think of other points that you need to use in comparing and contrasting a couple of stories.

The common points that you look for in each story are called a trait or an axis or an attribute. You will use trait or axis or attribute to compare and contrast the two houses of worship.

Continued on next page

Comparison and Contrast: Definitions, Continued

Comparison

In a comparison, you look at the **similarities** in the two places of worship. In this case, you consider how the two are alike.

Again, you compare the two houses of worship on a common trait, attribute, or axis, for example, the structure, how many buildings in the complex, etc. The number of buildings becomes the axis, trait, or attribute common to the two religious places.

Can you think of some other traits or attributes on which you might compare a couple of buildings?

Write a list of 8-10 common traits or attributes for buildings.

➢ Jot down your list of traits or attributes below.

1.

2.

3.

4.

5.

6.

7.

8.

Type of Similarities

Explicit Similarities. Sometimes similarities or likenesses are explicit; this means the similarities are clearly stated in the description.

- These similarities are easy to find; they might include color, size, or sound.
- The author states them up-front.

Implied or Implicit Similarities. Often, however, a similarity is not directly stated by the writer. It is implied.

- The similarity is not so easily to discover.
- The author may give you a number of clues about a similarity. You need to put the clues together to actually name the similarity.

When you compare St Euphemia with Suleymaniya Mosque, you need to look for both implicit and explicit similarities.

Continued on next page

Compare and Contrast: Definitions, Continued

Contrast

In contrast, you look for the **differences** between the two buildings.

➤ Differences show how they are **not** alike. They are dissimilar.

➤ As with comparisons, you need to have a common trait or axis on which to contrast two religious buildings.

Two Kinds of Contrast

As with comparison, some differences are explicit.

- You can usually find these explicit differences easily.
- They stand out.

There are also implicit differences between the items you are contrasting.

- You can find these from the clues that the author gives you.
- Since the clues may be scattered about in the description, you may need to wait until late in your reading to completely find an implicit difference.

As with comparison, you need to look for both implicit and explicit differences when you are contrasting the two religious buildings.

Find common traits in the two descriptions

Look back at the two descriptions.

➤ Find common traits or attributes on which you can compare them.

➤ List each trait in the table below.

➤ Check in which description the trait is discussed.

We have started the table on the next page. You complete it.

Find common traits in the two descriptions

Common Traits, Attributes, Axes

For St. Euphemia Church and Suleymaniya Mosque

Possible Traits, Attributes, Axes	Name of Building	
	St. Euphemia	Suleymaniya
Had an assembly place for worshipers	X	X
Was a religious complex of buildings		

The Thinking Organizer: Compare and Contrast St. Eufemia Church and Suleymaniya Mosque

Introduction

To help you compare and contrast the two religious buildings, you will use a **Compare and Contrast** thinking organizer. This thinking organizer should help you to:

- Keep the compare part and the contrast part of your work separate.

- Use the traits from table on the previous page to define the axes or traits for your comparison and contrast of two buildings.

- Get a "picture" or graphic list of comparison and contrast items to refer to when you write on comparing and contrasting the stories.

- Organize your work, making it easier to write a complete composition.

- See all you have written as well as the various parts.

Look at the thinking organizer

Look at the **COMPARE AND CONTRAST** thinking organizer that follows.

➢ Read each label or title on the organizer carefully.

➢ Then Read **Tips** which follow to help complete the organizer.

Continued on next page

The Thinking Organizer: Compare and Contrast St. Eufemia Church and Suleymaniya Mosque, Continued

Tips

Read these tips below carefully before you complete the organizer on the next page.

> ➤ Under **"Suleymaniya"**, write only about the mosque.
> ➤ Under **"St. Euphemia"**, write only about the structure of the church. These things are different from what you wrote under **"Suleymaniya"**.

What you write under "St. Euphemia" cannot be

the same as what you wrote under "Suleymaniya" and vice versa.

Important!

Look back at the axis table you completed earlier. It should give you the traits you can use in this comparison/contrast table.

The topic you write beside number 1 under Suleymaniya should be the same topic as you write beside number 1 under St. Euphemia. **Both should be a common trait or attribute.**

Look at the number 1's in the organizer,

what is the common attribute or axis of the number 1's?

That's right – It is the number of buildings?

> ➤ Under **"Both Places,"** write what is common or alike in both places of worship. The things you put under **"Both Places"** must occur in both St. Euphemia and in Suleymaniya.

We have started the comparison and contrast for you. You finish it up.

Compare and Contrast for St. Euphemia Church and Suleymaniya Mosque

Suleymaniya   **St. Euphemia**

Suleymaniya	Both Places	St. Euphemia
1. Has many buildings.	**Both Places**	1. Was one building.
2.	1. Have a large worship center.	2.
3.	2.	3.
4.	3.	4.
5.	4.	5.
6.	5.	6.

Write about the two places of worship

How to do it   Now write about the similarities and differences between St. Eufemia Church and Suleymaniya Mosque.

> ➤ Do not mix the similarities or the comparison with the contrast differences.

> ➤ Write the point of similarity or the likenesses of the two buildings first. This should be easy. You can probably put all the similarities in one or two paragraphs. Get them from the column on the previous page called **Both Places**.

> ➤ Do the differences in a different part of your writing. Don't mix them with the similarities.

> Here is where the axis, trait, and attribute are important. For example:

> > • The attribute such as the size of the complex is your general topic sentence.

> > • Then the specific information about St. Euphemia's size and Suleymaniya's size follows. They are two subordinate sentences to support the general topic sentence about size, which you first wrote.

Remember, put the attribute or trait that you contrast the two buildings on in your first sentence. It is the topic sentence for each contrast paragraph.

"Eadmer's Description of the Roman-Saxon Cathedral"

Another House of Worship

Below is a description of a Roman-Saxon cathedral in England. It is a little more complicated than the two you have just finished. Read it carefully, paying attention to the different parts of the cathedral.

Use the vocabulary below to help your understand new words:

crypt = a vault below the floor

confessionary = a place to confess to the priest

choir stall = place where the choir sang

cloisters = quiet, secluded courtyard where monks meditated

brothers = another name for monks

oratory = a place of prayer like a small chapel or a room for private praying

pontifical = pertaining to the Pope, the head of the Roman Catholic Church

---

This building was that very church which had been built by the Romans, and in some ways was a copy of St. Peter's. There were two altars in this Roman Saxon church: the great altar which was constructed of rough stones and mortar, close to the wall at the eastern end of the cathedral. The second altar was at a convenient distance in front of the great altar … At this altar … the priest conducted the daily service. The relics of many saints, including the head of St. Swithin, an Anglo Saxon saint, were placed in this altar.

To reach these two altars, you had to climb a crypt from the choir stall below. Under this crypt, was a confessionary. The vault of this confessionary was very high, requiring many steps to reach it. Beyond the choir stalls was the *aula* or body of the church, where the worshipers gathered.

[At] the middle of the aula were two towers which projected to the side of the aisles of the church. The south tower had an altar, which was dedicated to … Pope Gregory. At the side was the principal door of the church, which was and still is named *Suthdure*, (old English for "south door") This *Suthdure* is often mentioned by this name in the law-books of the ancient kings. Here all disputes from the whole kingdom, which couldn't legally be referred to the Kings Court or to the county courts were settled. ...

Continued on next page

"Eadmer's Description of the Roman-Saxon Cathedral", Continued

Opposite this south tower, on the north side of the aisles, there was another tower honoring St. Martin. This north tower had cloisters for the monks. As the south tower, mentioned above, was devoted to legal judgments of this world, in this north tower, the younger brothers were instructed in church knowledge.

At the extreme other end of the church from the great alter was the oratory of Mary. You had to climb up to this oratory. Once in the oratory, you could see the altar, at its eastern end, dedicated to Mary. Inside this altar was the head of St. Austroberta, another Anglo-Saxon martyr. When the priest conducted the service at this altar, he had his face turned to the east, towards the people who stood below in the aula.

This was the plan of the church of Canterbury, a Roman-Saxon church, which much later became the famous Canterbury Cathedral of Kent, England. ...

Adapted from:

"Appendix to Chapter I: Eadmer's Description of the Roman-Saxon Cathedral" in *Memorials of the Cathedral & priory of Christ in Canterbury* (1912) Author: Woodruff, C. Eveleigh (Charles Eveleigh), 1885 or 6-; Danks, William, 1845-1916. Not in copyright.

Mini-exercise   Do the study tables that follow. Read the directions in each table.

At the eastern end of the cathedral are _____ and _____ .

(Circle **the** letter that applies.)

a.	the oratory and a group of three saints' tombs.
b.	the little altar and the choir stalls.
c.	two courtyards.
d.	a great altar and a second altar.

Continued on next page

There are _____ ; one faces east, the other facing west.

(Circle **the** letter that applies.)

a.	two choir stalls
b.	two oratories
c.	two towers
d.	two cloisters

Write the answer to the question below.

List three activities that people did in the cathedral.

1.

_____

2.

_____

3.

_____

The place where people gathered for service was called _____.

(Circle **the** letter that applies.)

a.	the *assemblee*
b.	the *eglise*
c.	the *aula*
d.	the *narthex*

Classification   You are going to classify the activities that went on at St. Euphemia Church, Suleymaniya Mosque and at the Roman-Saxon cathedral. Before you start, you will learn about what classification is and how to use a thinking organizer to help you classify.

Defining classification: Triangles

Before you begin to classify the various human activities at the three houses of worship you have read about, let's do a little work on classification. To do this, look at the triangles below. They come in all shapes and sizes, but they have one thing in common: **All triangles have three sides.**

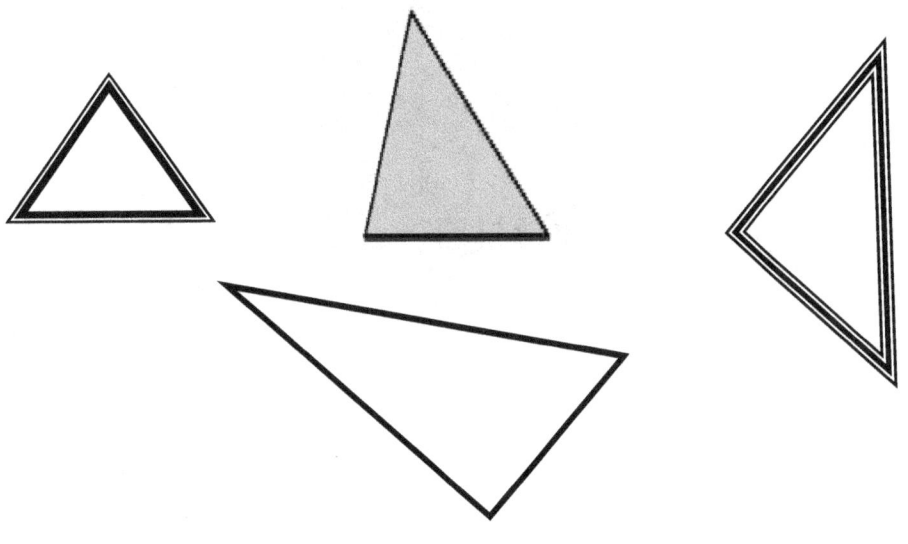

How to classify   How do you classify these various triangles?

The way to do this is to look for common traits or characteristics that will allow you to put the triangles into different groups or categories.

What are these traits or attributes to look at, in classifying triangles into categories? **The traits are angles and sides.** These are the two characteristics or traits that are common to all triangles. They define triangles.

Let's classify triangles by their sides. **All triangles can be classified by their sides.** Look at how triangles are classified by sides on the next page.

Continued on next page

Defining classification: Triangles, Continued

Classification by Sides

Type I: All sides are equal in length. Do you know what this kind of triangle is called? That's right: an **equilateral triangle**.

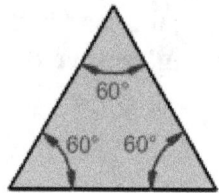

Type II: Two sides have the same length. This is called an **isosceles triangle**.

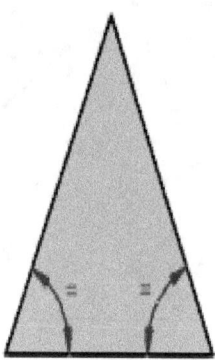

Type III: **No** sides are the same length. This is called a **scalene triangle**.

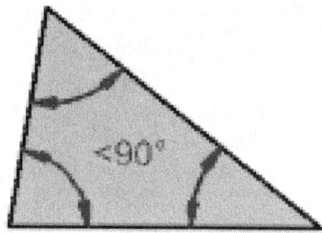

Continued on next page

Defining classification: Triangles, Continued

Important Tips

As you can see, this is one way to classify triangles. All triangles can fit into one of the categories: equilateral, isosceles, or scalene. This leads to some important information that you need to keep in mind.

- Each group of triangles -- equilateral, isosceles and scalene -- is called a **category**.

- The method of putting different triangles into these categories is called **classifying**.

- The total number of groups -- all the groups together -- form a **classification** or **system of classification**.

Quick Classification

➢ Get a sheet of paper.

Let's take vehicles: We will define them as four-wheeled vehicles:

➢ Write "**vehicle**" at the top of the sheet.

Now what groups can you think of that fit into this large group? Here's one: automobiles. Automobiles are a category of four-wheeled vehicles.

➢ Write the word *automobile* under **vehicle**. Leave space beside automobile for additional categories. Now think of three or four additional categories.

➢ Write your additional categories in a row beside automobiles. Leave space below each type of four-wheeled vehicle category as you are going to add to each of these groups.

➢ Okay, now fill out each category with as many types that fit under it as you can think of. For example one of the items that fit under automobiles is SUV. You can think of some others. Write them under automobile.

➢ Do the same for the other four-wheeled vehicle categories you just wrote.

What do you call this whole thing you have just done?

Use a thinking organizer to classify

Introduction

To help you classify, your will use a **CLASSIFICATION** thinking organizer.

- The organizer helps you to see the different categories and the traits or characteristics that are part of each category.

- You can also see all the "items" that belong to each category.

What a thinking organizer does

A thinking organizer should help you to:

- Keep the categories of your work separated.
- Define the characteristics or traits that you put under each category.
- Keep the items in each category where they belong.
- Get a complete picture of your system of classification. You can see your whole classification at a glance.
- Organize your written work and make it easier to write about a classification.
- See easily what you will write in your whole composition as well as its parts.

Thinking Organizer

➢ Look at the **CLASSIFICATION** thinking organizer on the next page.

➢ Read each label or title on the organizer carefully.

➢ Look at the organizer as you read the information that follows the thinking organizer. This information helps you understand how to use the organizer to classify.

Continued on next page

Use a thinking organizer to classify, Continued

The organizer below has been used to develop a classification for triangles.

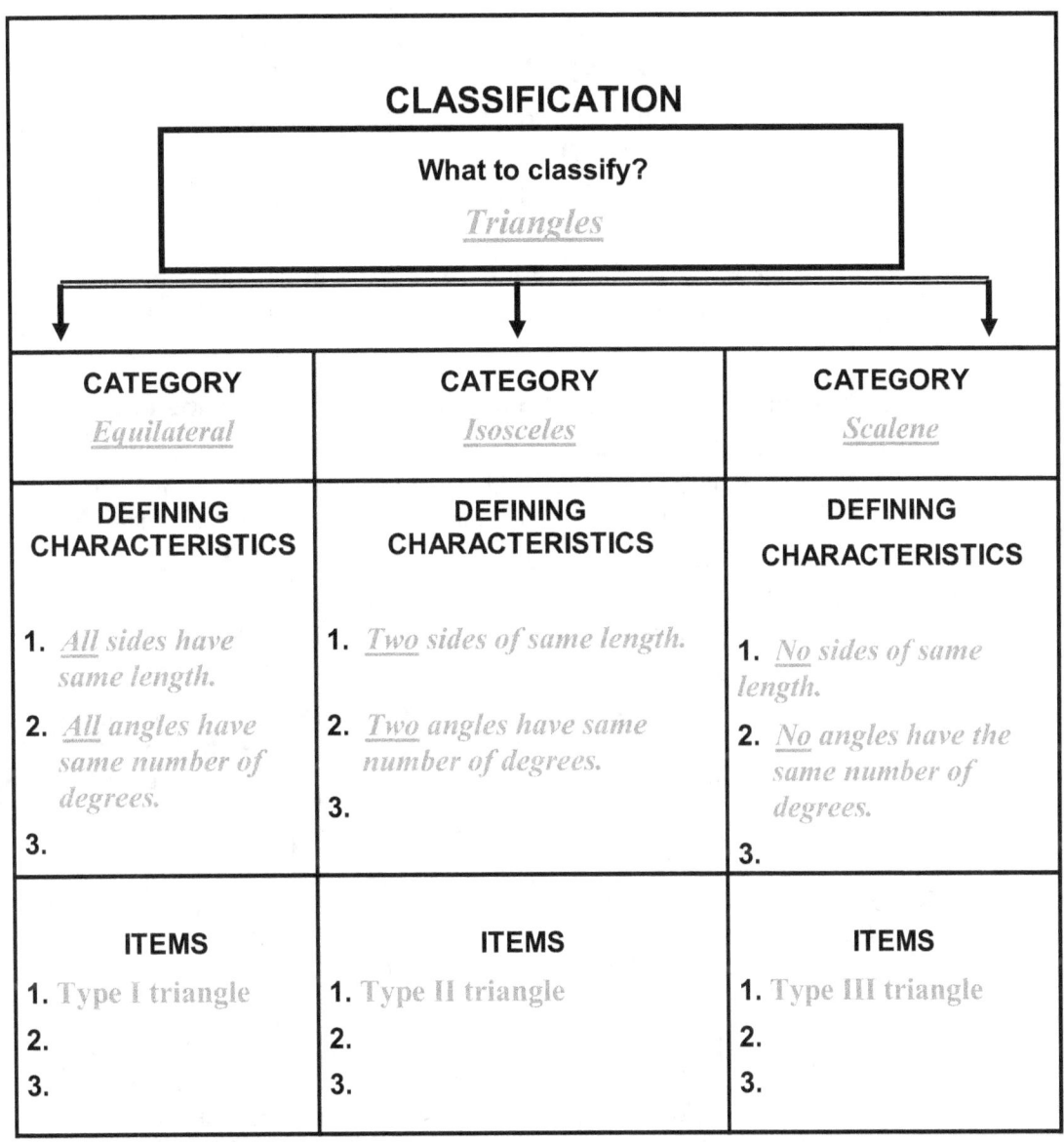

CLASSIFICATION

What to classify?

Triangles

CATEGORY	CATEGORY	CATEGORY
Equilateral	*Isosceles*	*Scalene*
DEFINING CHARACTERISTICS	**DEFINING CHARACTERISTICS**	**DEFINING CHARACTERISTICS**
1. *All sides have same length.* 2. *All angles have same number of degrees.* 3.	1. *Two sides of same length.* 2. *Two angles have same number of degrees.* 3.	1. *No sides of same length.* 2. *No angles have the same number of degrees.* 3.
ITEMS	**ITEMS**	**ITEMS**
1. Type I triangle 2. 3.	1. Type II triangle 2. 3.	1. Type III triangle 2. 3.

Continued on next page

Use a thinking organizer to classify, Continued

What thinking organizers do for writing!

You are going to use this thinking organizer to help you organize your work on categories and classification.

- The organizer gives you a picture of all the possible characteristics or traits of each category.

- It is like a record of your thoughts and ideas about your classification.

- It is a pictorial diagram you can refer to as you do your written work.

Refer to the **CLASSIFICATION** thinking organizer or diagram on the previous page as you read the information in the table below.

Part of Thinking Organizer	What it tells you	Tips or Hints
Title: **CLASSIFICATION**	The title tells you that you are going to use this organizer for: classifying.	Look at the top of the thinking organizer for this title
What to classify?	In this block, what has already been filled in?	For four-wheeled vehicles, what would you write in this block?
CATEGORY	What is written here for the triangle classification? What would you write in each **CATEGORY** for four-wheeled vehicles?	In each block under **CATEGORY**, write each main group.
DEFINING CHARACTERISTICS	What is listed under each **DEFINING CHARACTERISTICS** for the triangle classification?	Characteristics should fall into only one category, don't overlap, don't occur in other categories
ITEMS	What is listed in each **ITEMS** block in the triangle classification? Now write all the items you thought of, for the four-wheeled vehicles.	Each item has to have the **DEFINING CHARACTERISTICS** it is under.

Exclusivity

CATEGORY   A very important point about the categories you fill in the **CATEGORY** blocks:

- The **CATEGORY** in each block has to be exclusive.
- It cannot overlap with any other categories.
- Each **CATEGORY** has to stand by itself. It cannot depend on any other categories in your classification.

CHARAC-   The same thing is true about the characteristics you put in the
TERISTICS   **CHARACTERISTICS** you list: The traits or characteristics you list are exclusive just like the categories. The characteristics:

- Fall **only** in one specific category.
- Don't overlap with any other characteristics in any other category.
- Don't occur under the other categories of your classification.

Writing   Now that you have seen a couple of ways to categorize and classify, use your notes on four-wheeled vehicles to develop a classification for them. You:

- ➤ Put you notes about four-wheeled vehicles in the organizer that follows.
- ➤ Fill out the organizer with the categories and the items from your notes.
- ➤ Then fill in the distinguishing characteristics under each category.

We have started the organizer you finish it.

Classification of Four-Wheeled Vehicles

	What to classify?	
	4-wheeled vehicles	

CATEGORY	**CATEGORY**	**CATEGORY**
Automobiles		
DEFINING CHARACTERISTICS	**DEFINING CHARACTERISTICS**	**DEFINING CHARACTERISTICS**
1. *Primarily carry people* 2. *Usually have 4 doors* 3.	1. 2. 3.	1. 2. 3.
ITEMS	**ITEMS**	**ITEMS**
1. SUV 2. 3. 4.	1. 2. 3. 4.	1. 2. 3. 4

A Village Mosque

A poem about a mosque

Read the poem, "The Mosque" below.

> ➢ Pay attention to the structure of the mosque. Since this is a small village mosque, you can probably understand the parts of the building from it.

> ➢ Look at the human activities in this mosque. A lot of action that you may not expect is going on.

The Mosque
Richard Milnes

A SIMPLE unpartitioned [not divided up] room, —
Surmounted by an ample dome [with a dome on top],
Or, in some lands ...lie,
With centre open to the sky,

But roofed with arched cloisters round,
That mark the consecrated [religious worshipping] bound [area].
And shade the niche [corner] to Mecca turned,
By which two massive lights are burned;

With fountain fresh, where, ere [before] they pray,
Men wash the soil of earth away;

With shining minaret, thin and high.
From whose fine-trelliced [latticed] balcony
Announcement of the hours of prayer
Is uttered to the silent air;

The floor is spread with matting [mats and rugs] neat.
Unstained by touch of shodden [wearing shoes] feet —
A decent and delightful seat!

Continued on next page

A Village Mosque, Continued

The Mosque, continued

Here, after due devotions paid [prayers made],
… Men may in happy parlance [conversation] join,
And happy with serious thought combine;
May ask the news from lands far away,
May fix the business of to-day ; …

Children are running in and out
With silver-sounding laugh and shout,
No more disturbed in their sweet play,
No more disturbing those that pray,
Than the poor birds, that fluttering
Among the rafters there on high,
Or seek at times, with grateful pip [sounds birds make].
The corn fresh-sprinkled on the top. …

From: Richard Monckton Milnes, Baron. *The Poetical Works of Richard Monckton Milnes,* Volume: 1. Boston: Roberts Brothers. 1896. Not in copyright.

Before you continue, list below four activities that went on in this village mosque that were not mentioned in the other houses of worship you read about.

1.

2.

3.

4.

Classify activities at the houses of worship

Tips

You are going to classify all the activities that people do at St. Eufemia Church, Suleymaniya Mosque, the village mosque and at the Roman-Saxon cathedral described by Eadmer.

- ➢ Reread each description,

- ➢ Jot down the various activities that are mentioned in each description. Just write them in a list; don't try to put them into categories. In some cases, you will have to "suppose" about an activity, for example, when the choir stalls are mention, you know that people sang there. So one of activities is singing.

We have set up some basic categories for your classification. You need to fill out the following in your classification:

- ➢ Defining characteristics under each category.

- ➢ Writing in the items which are the specific activities you jotted down. Be sure to include the house of worship where the activity occurred.

Continued on next page

Classify activities at the houses of worship, Continued

CLASSIFICATION of Activities

What to classify?
Activities of people at the three houses of worship

CATEGORY *Activities of Priests and Monks*	CATEGORY **Activities of the People**	CATEGORY *Specialized Activities*
DEFINING CHARACTERISTICS 1. *Meditative* 2. 3. 4	**DEFINING CHARACTERISTICS** 1. 2. 3. 4	**DEFINING CHARACTERISTICS** 1. *Legal* 2. 3. 4.
ITEMS 1. *Preaching/Eadmer* 2. *Conducting services/ St. Eufemia, Suleymaniya, Eadmer* 3. 4. 5.	**ITEMS** 1. 2. 3. 4. 5.	**ITEMS** 1. *Hold court/Eadmer* 2. 3. 4. 5.

Classify activities at the houses of worship, Continued

Writing

Now that you have completed the **CLASSIFICATION** thinking organizer for the various activities at St. Euphemia Church, Suleymaniya Mosque, Eadmer's Roman-Saxon cathedral and at the village mosque:

> ➢ Write about the various activities.

> ➢ Refer back to the thinking organizer and to the four descriptions to support your writing.

> ➢ Remember to use all the material in the organizer to give a complete picture of the activities.

Think about and summarize	What kinds of thinking organizers did you use in this chapter? Which were easy to use? Which, difficult?
	Now write a brief summary about using thinking organizers. You could include the answers to the questions above. Think of some other important points.　　　　　　　　　　　(Do your writing below.)

Preview

The Builders

Who built the places of worship which you have just read about? Clearly, Suleymaniya Mosque was built by Sinan, who was a servant of the sultan.

Originally, Sinan was born into a Christian family. During his life time, The Ottoman Turks ruled much of the Middle East. As a child, Sinan was snatched by the sultan's soldiers and taken to Istanbul, which was the capital of the Ottoman empire. Here he was forced to become a Muslim and serve in the sultan's elite corps, the Janissaries.

Sinan had a brilliant career in this service as an architect for the sultan. As a Janissary, Sinan built some of the most beautiful and majestic buildings for the Ottomans.

As for the village mosque and Eadmer's Roman-Saxon cathedral, we don't know who were the architects of those houses of worship.

Topic to cover

In the next chapter, you will read some folktales about strange creatures who people thought might have helped to build churches.

Chapter II
The Devil's in the Making

Introduction and Overview

Demons and Houses of Worship

Are you surprised? The devil and places of worship – together they just don't make sense. Well, as you will see, there are many stories about how devils were involved with churches.

What to do: Lesson Objectives

➢ Using a **Cause and Effect** thinking organizer, define cause and effect in The Tale of Trondenes Church.

➢ Based on a grammar exercise, use a style with complex sentences to write about comparison and contrast.

Companion Guide

This workbook is a companion to *"Snipp snapp snute, så er eventyret ute" – Folklore Reader and Critical Thinking Workbook*, which has additional critical thinking materials and selections.

Lesson Content

The selections to read are:

- "Asmodeus and Solomon" by Louis Ginzburg.
- "The Tale of Trondenes Church" from Norway.
- "The Devil's Church Building" from Estonia.

Solomon and the Demon Asmodeus

Introduction   Solomon, as you know, was one of ancient Israel's most famous rulers. He was noted for his wisdom.

- This religious folk tale is from the "Testament of Solomon." It is also found in a number of other ancient sources.
- In the "r"eligious folk tale that follows, King Solomon has a problem. Read how he solves it.

"Asmodeus and Solomon"
Louis Ginzburg

While Solomon was occupied with building his temple, he had great difficulty in devising [finding] ways of fitting the stone from the quarry into the building, for the Torah [the Jewish holy book] explicitly prohibits ... [using] iron tools in erecting an altar.

... Scholars told him that Moses had used the shamir, the stone that splits rocks, to engrave the names of the tribes on the precious stones of the signet worn by the high priest. [No one, not even demons] could give the king any information as to where the shamir could be found. [The demons] thought that Asmodeus, king of demons, knew the secret [of the shamir], and they told Solomon the name of the mountain on which Asmodeus dwelled.

On this mountain there was a well from which Asmodeus obtained [got] his drinking water. He closed it up daily with a large rock and sealed it before going to heaven, where he went every day to take part in the discussions in the heavenly academy. [From the heavenly academy] Asmodeus descended again to earth ... to be present, though invisible, at the debates in the [schools and academies on earth]. Then, after investigating the seal on the well to ... [see] if it had been tampered with, he drank from [its] water.

Solomon sent his chief, Benaiah ... to capture Asmodeus. To help Banaiah, Solomon [gave] him ... a chain with a ring on which the Name of God was engraved, a bundle of wool, and a skin [filled with] wine.

When he arrived at the well, Benaiah drew [out all] the water from the well through a hole he bored [in the bottom of the well]. ... Having stopped up the hole with the wool, he filled the well with wine from above.

Continued on next page

Solomon and the Demon Asmodeus, Continued

When Asmodeus descended from heaven, to his ... [surprise], he found wine instead of water in the well, although everything else seemed untouched. At first, he would not drink any wine and cited the Bible verses that [are] ... against drinking wine, to inspire himself with moral courage. [But] then, Asmodeus succumbed [gave in] to his consuming thirst, and drank ... until his senses were overpowered, and he fell into a deep sleep.

Benaiah, watching him from a tree, then came, and drew [put] the chain about Asmodeus' neck. The demon, on awakening, tried to free himself, but Benaiah called to him: "The Name of thy Lord is upon thee." ... Thus, Asmodeus then permitted himself to be led off without resisting.

When Solomon asked him about the shamir, Asmodeus told Solomon that the shamir was given by God to the angel of the sea, and that angel entrusted none with the shamir except the moor hen, which had taken an oath to watch the shamir carefully. The moor hen takes the shamir with her to [uninhabited] mountains, ... splits rocks there with it and sows seeds. ... Then men can live on these formerly barren mountains.

Solomon then sent one of his servants to seek the [bird's] nest ... and [to] lay a piece of glass over the nest. When the moor hen came and could not reach her young, she flew away and fetched the shamir to use it on the glass. Then the man shouted and so terrified the moor hen that she dropped the shamir and flew away. [In this way] Solomon's man ... [got hold] of the shamir, and [took] ... it to Solomon. ... Thus Solomon was able to complete his temple with the help of Asmodeus, king of the demons.

Adapted from: Ginzberg, Louis. *Legends of the Jews*, Volume IV, translated by Henrietta Szold, Paul Radin, et al. Philadelphia: The Jewish Publication Society of America, 1901. Not in copyright. At: http://www.archive.org/details/legendsofjews04ginz

---

Mini-exercise   Complete the study tables. Follow the directions in each table.

Continued on next page

Solomon and the Demon Asmodeus, Continued

What was the *shamir*?

(Circle **the letter** that applies.)

a.	A piece of a diamond used to split stones and rocks.
b.	A laser-lie light to split stones.
c.	A stone guarded by a moor hen.
d.	A stone found in a temple.

What would you call the *shamir*?

(Circle **the letter** that applies.)

a.	A kitchen tool.
b.	A magical weapon.
c.	A wonderful instrument.
d.	A stone found in a temple.

The Gnome Who built a Church

A Tale from Norway

This folk tale is about a priest who made a bargain with a devil-figure. He thought he was going to lose to the "devil," but at the last moment, he won.

"Tale of Trondenes Church"

One night, many hundred years ago, a priest from Trondenes in the northern part of Norway wandered about wondering how he could build a church for his parishioners. Since the congregation was small and all were poor, it just didn't seem possible. He had already decided where the church should stand and had come to the exact spot that night. While the priest stood and looked at the mountains in the moonlight, he caught sight of a gnome coming toward him. Now this priest was not the least bit afraid. When the gnome asked what he was about so late at night, the priest answered that he wished to build his parishioners a church, but just couldn't manage it. The gnome didn't see a problem with that. He proposed that they make an agreement: "If you can get me the moon in the mountain, we will build you a church as tall as you please."

"Done," agreed the priest happily. He showed the gnome where he should build the church and told him the day or night (Gnomes and trolls like demons are afraid of daylight) that the building should be finished.

Every night the priest went out to the cliff where the church was being built. The work was going fabulously fast although the priest never saw a single person at the site.

Then the priest began to be a bit afraid, wondering how in the world he could get the moon he had promised the gnome. Late one night, the church was almost finished. The priest wandered out to the cliff. He was still wondering how he would fulfill his promise, for tonight the church would be completed. Then he suddenly heard a woman's voice singing from the mountains:

> **"Hush, hush my child,**
> **Now you must sleep soon;**
> **Tomorrow papa Dagfinn comes**
> **with the moon."**

When the priest heard the name *Dagfinn*, he knew he had been saved because gnomes and trolls die when they hear someone say their name.

Think about: Knowing that gnomes are afraid of daylight, why might Dagfinn want to have the moon?

Continued on next page

The Gnome Who built a Church, Continued

The priest went to the church. He saw a golden globe set on the church spire. The gnome was up there. So the priest yelled up at the gnome on the spire, "Hey, you, Dagfinn, be careful that you don't fall down."

At that very moment, the church spire collapsed, and there was a crashing and banging in the mountains like you wouldn't believe. A voice called out: "On the Sunday before All Saints Day, the whole church will collapse and bury the congregation."

In spite of repeated attempts, people have never succeeded in getting the spire back on the church, and the spire today still stands away from the church. Below the church yard, in the mountains there are abandoned wagons that were used in building the church. You can see three figures in stone down there too. Who can they be?

From: http://www.intermedia.uio.no/ariadne/Kulturhistorie/kulturhistorisk-informasjonsbank/sagn/vandresagnkatalogen/ml7050-ml8025-historiske-sagn/7065/7065-1138.html/

ML7065-1138 Sagnet om Trondeneskirken.   (Translated by David Garnett)

Define cause and effect

What to do You are going to explore this folktale for cause and effect.

> ➤ You will do this by filling out a new thinking organizer.
>
> ➤ Before you begin, you will read a bit about cause and effect.
>
> ➤ Begin with the section on the next page called **Some Examples**.

Continued on next page

Define cause and effect, Continued

Some Examples   Rather than give a definition of cause and effect, you will explore some examples. Look at the table below. It has some examples to help explain causes and effects.

Cause(s)	Effect(s)
• **Lightning** • **Thunder** • **Strong wind**	**A storm is brewing.**
Eat a big tub of buttery and salted popcorn	• **Get thirsty … drink soda** • **Feel stuffed**
Slip on the ice and fall on your tush	• **Hurt yourself** • **Look very foolish**
• **Red, yellow and brown leaves** • **Geese and ducks flying south** • **Thanksgiving is coming**	**Winter is on the way.**
• **Sand** • **Camels** • **Hot sun and dry wind** • **Palm and date trees at an oasis**	**You're in a desert.**

Continued on next page

Define cause and effect, Continued

An easy way to state cause and effect is to use an *If ... then* sentence. Some examples are below.

➢ We have mixed up the cause-effect statements below; now you match the cause with its correct effect.

➢ Draw lines from the cause to the proper effect. Remember, each sentence must make sense and be logical.

Cause(s)	Effect(s)
If I run hardest of all,	then someone will get angry with me.
If we play fair,	my team will win.
If I smack my dog,	my TV won't work well.
If the weather is freezing and icy,	then cars on I-95 will slip and slide.
If there are a lot of sunspots,	I'll probably win the race.

Continue on next page

46

Define cause and effect, Continued

Now you try it. Below is a blank cause-effect table. Fill it in with causes and effects. Remember, **Cause 1.** corresponds to number **Effect 1**, etc.

Cause(s)	Effect(s)
1.	1.
2.	2.
3.	3.
4.	4.
5.	5.

Use a Cause and Effect organizer with Trondenes Church

What to do Now that you have a better understanding of cause and effect, fill in the **Cause and Effect** organizer that follows to help you find causes and their effects in the "Tale of Trondenes Church." Read **Tips** first.

Continued on next page

Use a Cause and Effect **organizer with** Trondenes Church,
Continued

Tips for Cause and Effect in "The Tale of Trondenes Church"

Step	What you do
1	Beside each number in a Cause(s) block, write, in your own words, a cause from the folktale.
2	Beside the same number in the Effect(s) box, write in your own words an effect for that cause. Note: Remember, the number of a cause must correspond to the same number of an effect. We have started the organizer. You complete it.

CAUSE AND EFFECT: "The Tale of Trondenes Church"

Cause(s)

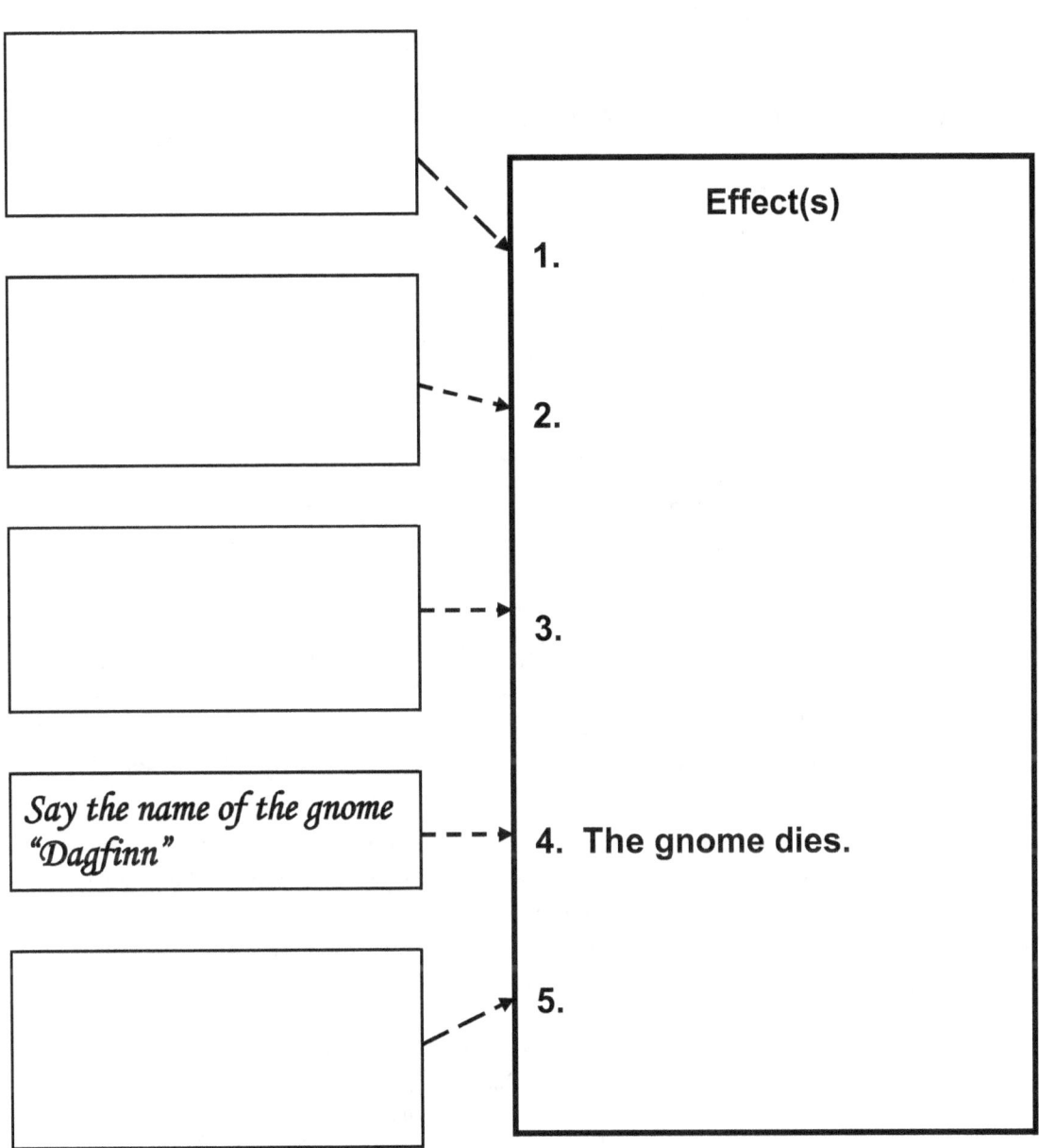

Effect(s)

1.

2.

3.

4. **The gnome dies.**

5.

(Cause box 4): *Say the name of the gnome "Dagfinn"*

Continued on next page

49

Cause and Effect: Trondenes Church, Continued

Writing Now write about the causes and effects you found in the "Tale of Trondenes Church." Be sure to give examples from the tale and use the organizer you have just completed.

The Devil and a Church in Estonia

Background Estonia is a country on the Baltic Sea. It is north of Latvia and east of Finland, not far from Scandinavia. The people were once part of the former Soviet Union. Their language is related to Finnish.

Now, read this folktale about the devil, who made a bargain. Unlike the priest of Trondenes Church, this demon couldn't keep his bargain.

"The Devil's Church Building"

The devil wanted to marry the daughter of a famous man. He went to the girl's father to ask for her hand, but the man said to the devil: "I won't give you my daughter – no way – unless you first build a stone church on top of the mountain – in one night!"

So the devil began to work one evening. He worked half the night, but only succeeded in getting half the wall of the church done. Soon the cock would crow. The devil realized that he wouldn't get the church finished, so in his frustration, he began to tear down the wall he had just completed, throwing the stones all over the place.

Some of the wall, however, remained in place, and you can see it today. At the foot of the mountain, there are loose stones lying around. On all these stones are fingerprints of the devil, where he took hold of the stones as he was throwing them down the mountain. Since that wedding was postponed, the devil has never again let himself be seen.

Adapted from: Email-Zusendung von Hiiemäe, Reet vom Estnischen Literaturmuseum, Tartu, im April 2002
Aus: Muistendid Vanapaganast. [Die Sagen über den dummen Teufel.]
Monumenta Estoniae Antiquae II. Eduard Laugaste und Ellen Liiv (Hrsg). Tallinn 1970, S. 125, Nr. 148. Not in copyright
From: http://www.sagen.at/index.html   (Translated by David Garnett)

50

Compare and contrast the two church-building folk tales

Do you remember this organizer?

You have already used a couple of thinking organizers to compare and contrast. The organizer that follows should be familiar to you. If not, refer back to **Chapter I**, to review it.

The Gnome

Devil who wanted to marry

1. lived in Norway.

2.

3.

4.

5.

6.

Both of them

1. Made a bargain.

2.

3.

4.

5.

1. From Estonia.

2.

3.

4.

5.

6.

Compare and contrast the two church-building folk tales, Continued

A Little Help
Before you start to write about the similarities and differences between these two folk tales, let's look at the style of writing you might use to write about them. First look at the short paragraph below contrasting two folklore heroes.

Essa and Wilhelm Tell are different too. Essa was a young boy. Tell was a married man. Essa lived in Finland. Tell lived in Switzerland. Tell became a national hero of his country. Essa never became famous. Tell killed Gessler, who made him suffer. Essa didn't kill anyone. Essa shot an apple off his grandfather's head. Tell shot his apple off his son's head.

Mini- exercise
To help you understand the above writing style about Tell and Essa, do the study tables below.

The main problem with the paragraph above is that:

(Circle **only** one answer.)

a.	the sentences are very long.
b.	there are too many complicated words in the sentences.
c.	the sentences are short. The style is choppy.
d.	there is a lot of repetition in the sentences.

To correct the problem, I would: (Choose **all** answers that apply.)

a.	Combine some of the short sentences.
b.	Drop a lot of the complex words and phrases.
c.	Use contrasting phrases like *on the contrary* in other sentences.
d.	Check the punctuation in all the sentences above.

Continued on next page

Compare and contrast the two church-building folk tales, Continued

Revised Paragraph

Look at the revised paragraph below. Then complete the study tables after the revised paragraph to help you understand how the style was changed.

Essa and Wilhelm Tell are different too. Essa was a teenager **while** Tell was a married man. Essa lived in Finland. Tell lived in Switzerland. Tell became a national hero of his country. **On the other hand,** Essa never became famous in his country. Tell killed Gessler, who made him suffer; Essa didn't kill anyone. Essa shot an apple off his grandfather's head, **but** Tell shot the apple off his own son's head.

Mini-exercise

Look, again, at the revised paragraph above. Then complete the study table below

From the list in the table, check the box(s) beside the revisions that were applied to the original paragraph.

Revision Table for the Essa-Tell Paragraph

	Many complex words were added to the original paragraph.
	Some short sentences were combined into one longer sentence.
	Punctuation was changed.
	Words like *but* and *on the other hand* were used to highlight a contrast.

Continued on next page

Compare and contrast the two church-building folk tales, Continued

Writing

> ➤ Review the **Compare and Contrast** thinking organizer for the two churches, the one in Estonia and the other in Norway.

> ➤ Then write about the similarities and differences between the two.

> ➤ Be sure to use you thinking organizer.

> ➤ Refer back to the two tales to support your writing.

Chapter III
Martyrs

Introduction and Overview

Martyrs

What is a martyr? We will not define the term for you; rather, you are going to read about various religious people who are considered martyrs.

As you read, you will build your own picture of a martyr so that at the end of this chapter you can write about your own complete idea of what a martyr is.

What to do: Lesson Objectives

You will:

➢ Define, in your own terms, what a martyr is, from the various selections in the chapter.

➢ Use some important thinking organizers, together with the selections about martyrs, to help organize your thinking before you write.

Companion Guide

This workbook is a companion to *"Snipp snapp snute, så er eventyret ute" – Folklore Reader and Critical Thinking Workbook*, which has additional critical thinking materials and reading selections.

Continued on next page

Introduction and Overview, Continued

Lesson Components

A text or group of texts that you will read. Most of the writing and other work you do require you to read and refer to these text resource(s).

Any of a number of activities or exercises which you need to complete. These activities may include:

- Vocabulary exercises.
- Questions to answer.
- Study tables to complete
- Thinking organizers (graphic or picture diagrams) to fill out.
- Written work to plan, organize, and write.

All these activities should help you to read and understand the texts or to write about them.

You may have to complete a project, which requires limited research.

Lesson Content

The selections are about people who gave themselves completely to their religion in some unique way:

- "Hus at the Stake" by FyodorTyutchev, a Russian poet.
- Papus and Lulianus, two Jewish martyrs from the Roman Empire.
- Maurice and his legionnaires, radical soldiers, who calmly and faithfully stood their ground.
- "Torgjus' Daughters" - Little Kari, who would rather die than submit, from Norway.
- "The Musician's Tale: King Olaf's Saga," by Henry Wadsworth Longfellow.

Burned at the Stake!

A Bit of Background
In the late 15th and early 16th centuries, the Roman Catholic Church, located at the Vatican in Rome, Italy, was in charge of the only religion in Western Europe: Roman Catholicism.

There were some Catholics who felt that the Vatican had many faults. Some, like a famous Dutch thinker in Holland called Erasmus, hoped to reform or change the Roman Catholic Church from within.

Others eventually broke with the Roman Catholic Church in a movement called Protestantism or the Protestant Reformation. The people of this movement were called Protestants (those who protest).

The leader of this reformation was a former German Catholic priest named Martin Luther. Jan Hus, the subject of the poem below, was also a Protestant. He brought Protestantism to the Czech people, who were part of the Austrian empire at that time. Most of the Austrians, who ruled the Czechs, were Roman Catholics.

Let's get started
As you read the poem, "Hus at the Stake," jot down the kinds of people attending his burning.

---

356. Hus at the Stake
Tyuchev

The pyre [pile of wood] has been built. The fateful
flame's about to flare and all is silent,
save for gentle crackles as deep within the pyre
the treacherous fire filters.

Crowding, people are fanned by darting smoke.
All are here, unlearned folk,
here the oppressed and the oppressor,
violence and falsehood: knights and clergy,

Continued on next page

57

Burned at the Stake!, Continued

Here the treacherous kaiser [German emperor] here the high assembly
of imperial and spiritual princes,
and he himself, the hierarchy of Rome [the Pope],
sinful in infallibility.

She's here too, simple old woman,
unforgotten since those times,
crossing herself and sighing,
bringing, like a penny, her kindling [wood] to the pyre.

Like a sacrificial offering,
your great and righteous man before us all,
already fanned by fiery brilliance [the flames of the fire],
praying, voice untrembling,

This sacred teacher of the Czechs, Jan Hus,
unwavering [firm] witness to Christ,
stern exposer of Vatican lies,
in all his high simplicity,

Betraying neither God nor his own people,
undefeated, battling on
for holy truth and for His [Jesus'] freedom,
for everything which Rome called heresy [preaching against the Roman Catholic Church.]

In spirit Hus is in Heaven, in family love
he's here still, among his people,
shining, knowing that it was his blood
which flowed defending the blood of Christ. …

http://www.pereplet.ru/moshkow/LITRA/TUTCHEW/english.html

Continued on next page

Burned at the Stake!, Continued

Mini-exercise   Do the study tables below. Follow the directions in each table.

List below ten different types of people who gathered to watch Hus' burning:

1.	
2.	
3.	
4.	
5.	
6.	
7.	
8.	
9.	
10.	

The emperor in the poem represents _____ over the Czechs.

(Circle **the** letter that applies.)

a.	the religious authority
b.	the educational authorities
c.	the ruling authority
d.	the mythological authority

Continued on next page

Burned at the Stake, Continued

Rome and the Vatican are _____ over the Czechs.

(Circle **the** letter that applies.)

a.	the civil authority
b.	the religious authority
c.	the police authority
d.	the social authority

What might the old woman represent?

(Circle **the** letter that applies.)

a.	The homeless.
b.	Poor people.
c.	Farmers who lost their land.
d.	The rich and well-off.

Jan Hus believed he was defying [against] _____

(Circle **all the letters** that apply.)

a.	the Roman Catholic pope who was in charge of the Czechs' religion.
b.	the emperor and nobles ruling the Czechs.
c.	the believers in God.
d.	Jesus.

Look at the people in Tyutchev's poem

An Old Friend   Look at the **Classification** thinking organizer on the next page. You used it in the last chapter. If you can't remember it, reread the section in **Chapter I** which tells how to use this organizer.

We have started to classify the people in the poem. You finish the organizer.

Continued on next page

Look at the people in Tyutchev's poem, Continued

CLASSIFICATION of People in "Hus at the Stake"

What to classify?
People in the poem

CATEGORY	CATEGORY	CATEGORY
Rich and Powerful		*Poor Folk*
DEFINING CHARACTERISTICS	**DEFINING CHARACTERISTICS**	**DEFINING CHARACTERISTICS**
1. *Wealth*	1.	*1. No money*
2.	2.	2.
3.	3.	3.
4	4	4.
ITEMS	**ITEMS**	**ITEMS**
1. *Emperor*	1.	*1. Old Woman*
2.	2.	2.
		3.
3.	3.	4.
4.	4.	5.
	5.	

Continued on next page

Look at the people in Tyutchev's poem, Continued

Write about the people and Jon Hus

Now that you have looked at the different kinds of people in "Hus at the Stake," write about the people.

➤ Use the categories as part of the topic sentence, one in each paragraph.
➤ Next, write the defining characteristics under each category, in sentences. These characteristics will explain about the kind of person of the category.
➤ Last, as examples of each category, use the people you listed under the items of each category.

When you write about the people, try to give a little information about them, for example,

- their place in society,

- how they might have felt about Jan Hus, the Protestant,

- how they might have behaved while watching Hus' burning.

Your last paragraph should be one defining trait or characteristic of a martyr that you got from Jon Hus himself. You only need to discuss one characteristic that defines Hus as a martyr.

➤ Write the characteristic or trait in the topic sentence.
➤ Then write three or four supporting sentences discussing where Hus actually shows this trait.

Remember to save your work about the martyr trait of Jon Hus as you will use it later in this chapter.

Sacrificed!

Introduction

The short tale that follows is about two Jewish martyrs during the time that the Roman Empire ruled Israel and Canaan.

> ➢ Remember, look for new traits that will help you build your idea of what martyrs are and how they act.

"World of the Sages: Pious Papus"
Levi Cooper

The wicked Roman government once issued an edict against the Jewish people prohibiting the study of the Torah [the Jewish holy book]. Rabbi Akiva disobeyed this injunction [prohibition] and publicly convened assemblies where he [read and] taught Torah.

… It was not long before Rabbi Akiva was arrested and thrown into prison for [reading] Torah. As he sat in jail, Papus [one of his close associates] was thrown in, with him. Rabbi Akiva exclaimed: "Papus, what has brought you here … ?"

Rabbi Akiva was … aware that Papus had not dared to defy the Roman edict against Torah study and was surprised to find that his friend had been arrested too. Without answering the question, Papus bemoaned [complained about] his fate: "Fortunate are you, Rabbi Akiva, for you were apprehended [arrested] because you read the Torah. [I was arrested for] meaningless matters."

"So what are these 'meaningless matters'?" asked Rabbi Akiva.

"The daughter of a Roman emperor was found dead, and the Romans accused the Jews of killing her and threatened [to punish] the entire Jewish population. Well, Rabbi, you know my brother Lulianus and I, we stepped up to take sole responsibility for this crime. But we had not kill the child." exclaimed Papus.

"Ah," thought Rabbi Akiva, "what a courageous act: To save the Jewish people from a Roman … [massacre or pogrom]!"

Before you continue with the tale, do the study table below.

Papus calls his act "meaningless matters." This shows that Papus:
(Circle **all** that apply.)

    a. **doesn't understand what he has done.**
    b. **is humble about his actions.**
    c. **is dumb and foolish.**
    d. **expects the rabbi to praise him.**

Continued on next page

Sacrificed!, Continued

When Papus and Lulianus were later brought before the Roman governor, Turyanus, in the city of Lod, Turyanus laughed at them and mockingly said, "If you are from the nation of Hananya, Mishael and Azarya, let your God come and save you from my hand, as He saved them [from the fires in the furnace where] Nebuchadnezzar had thrown them!"

Papus and Lulianus replied:

> **"Hananya, Mishael and Azarya were righteous ... and were worthy of that a miracle [that saved them from the fire]. ... Remember, Nebuchadnezzar was a fair king who deserved those miracles he [caused] because when the three boys emerged from the furnace unharmed, he praised the Almighty for the miracle. You, Turyanus, evil one, are a mere commoner, not worthy of any miracle. ... If you do not kill us, the Omnipresent [Jehovah] has many executioners, and the Omnipresent has many bears and lions in this world ... [that] could attack ... and kill us."**

The brothers then concluded: "The only reason that Jehovah placed us in your hand is to eventually avenge our blood from your hand!"

Turyanus became very angry at these words, so he had the two brothers killed.

As [people] stood staring in stunned silence at the slain bodies of the two brothers, with blood still dripping from the sword of Turyanus - a pair of officers arrived from Rome with an imperial edict [order of the emperor] against Turyanus. The messengers promptly clubbed Turyanus to death, thus fulfilling the brothers' prediction of being avenged for their deaths.

Adapted from:
http://www.jpost.com/servlet/Satellite?pagename=JPost%2FJPArticle%2FShowFull&cid=1245184867591. Not in copyright

---

Mini-exercise   Do the study tables that follow. Follow the directions in each table.

Continued on next page

Sacrificed!, Continued

How does Papus and Lulianus' "crime" compare to Rabbi Akiva's?

(Write your answer below.)

Explain how Papus and Lulianus "got revenge" on Turyanus:

(Write your answer below.)

Continued on next page

Sacrificed!, Continued

Find the martyr in Papus and Lulianus

You are going to write about the martyr traits or characteristics of Papus and Lulianus. You already began this when you answered the question about the difference between the two brothers and Rabbi Akiva.

You will use the **Character Trait** table that follows to help you explore the possible traits that make Papus and Lulianus martyrs. Read **Tips** below to help you fill out the table on the next page.

Tips

Compare Papus and Lulianus to Rabbi Akiva using the table on the next page.

➤ In the column called **Possible Character Traits,** list a character trait that you think makes a person a martyr. (Papus gives you a number of clues.)

➤ Then check the *Papus and Lulianus* box if they have the trait.

➤ If Rabbi Akiva has one of these traits, check the box under his name too.

➤ We have started the traits and checked some boxes. You think of other traits and complete the table.

Find the martyr in Papus and Lulianus

Character Table for
Papus and Lulianus

Possible Character Traits	Person	
	Papus and Lulianus	Rabbi Akiva
Bravery	X	X
Wisdom		X
Makes the ultimate sacrifice: dying	X	

Continued on next page

Find the martyr in Papus and Lulianus, Continued

Writing

Write about how Papus and Lulianus were martyrs.

> ➢ Discuss each trait from the table you have just completed.
>
> As you write, explain how the two brothers showed or exhibited the trait.

> ➢ It may help you to show the way that Rabbi Akiva was different from the two brothers and may not have shown or done things that that they did.

> ➢ Be sure to discuss the ultimate sacrifice that the two brothers made.

**Save your writing on Papus and Lulianus
You will use it later in this chapter.**

Radical Soldiers

A Little Background

In the first century CE, the Roman Empire dominated all of Europe and much of the Middle East. Much of the empire's time was spent in conquering and subduing the various peoples and tribes whose lands the Romans wanted to incorporate into their empire.

The story you are going to read is about a contingent of empire soldiers who were sent to help subdue an uprising in Gaul (modern France). Most of the Romans and the peoples they ruled over were **not** Christians, but pagans. These soldiers were an exception.

What to look for

Again, as you read this tragic story,

> ➢ Look for the characteristics or traits that make these Roman soldiers, known as legionnaires, martyrs.

> ➢ Keep a list of the possibilities.

Continued on next page

Radical Soldiers, Continued

Maurice and the Theban Legion -- Martyrs, Soldiers, Radicals

Maurice, an officer of the Roman legions and a Christian, was sent to fight for the Roman emperor in Gaul [modern France]. He went with his men to the place where the battle was … [to take place]. His men were [called] the Theban Legion of the Roman Army. The legion … [consisted] of almost all Christians from Northern Egypt … .

The [Theban Legion under Maurice] had … been called to battle to put down a peasant [farmers'] revolt. The peasants had grown tired of being oppressed and abused by the Roman Empire and had begun to resist the Romans. They were known as the *bagaudae*, and they were the reason that the Theban legion (all 6,600 of them) had been called to Gaul.

When [Maurice and his troops] arrived, they discovered two things that made them balk [stop]: They were being asked to make war on peasants, and they were asked to make a sacrifice to the Roman gods on the night before the battle. Maurice and his legion resisted both of these requests. They continued to proclaim their Christian faith and refused to sacrifice to the Roman gods even [though] they were threatened … .

Finally, the emperor ordered the decimation [destruction] of the legion. … All 6,600 men were lined up and every tenth soldier was murdered. 660 men died because they refused to … follow the emperor's orders. The remaining men were asked again if they would make a sacrifice to the pagan gods to spare their own lives. When the [remainder of the] legion refused, they [too were slaughtered].

As these members of the Theban legion were [killed], some of the troops tasked with executing them were converted by the Thebans' nonviolent resistance. Even though the men of the Theban legion held weapons, they allowed themselves to be killed, without defending themselves. Each murder made a strong statement about the inability of the Roman Empire to win the heart and will of the soldiers of the Theban legion. ...

Before you continue with the story, write you answer to the question below:
**How do you think it felt to be a Christian soldier fighting in a pagan army?
What might be some of the problems?**

_____

Continued on next page

Radical Soldiers, Continued

Maurice offered some words to his superiors and to the emperor:

> **"We are your soldiers, but we are also servants of the true God. We owe you military service and obedience; but we cannot renounce Him who is our Creator and Master, and also yours, even though you reject Him. In all things which are not against His law we most willingly obey you, as we have done hitherto [up to now]. …We have taken an oath to God before we took one to you; you can place no confidence in our second oath if we violate the first....We have seen our companions slain without lamenting them, and we rejoice at their honor. Neither this nor any other provocation [threat] has tempted us to revolt. We have arms in our hands, but we do not resist because we could rather die innocent than live by any sin."**

After this, the emperor ordered the slaughter of the remaining … soldiers. They stood quietly and allowed their executioners to take their lives. Though it cost them their lives, the Theban legion maintained the faith that held them to a higher calling than the [Roman] Empire.

Adapted from: http://www.ttstm.com/2009/09/september-22-maurice-and-theban-legion.html

---

Mini-exercise   Complete the study tables. Follow the directions in each table.

The main thing the Theban soldiers refused to do was to ------------ .

(Circle **the** letter that applies.)

a.	eat pork on Saturday
b.	worship the Roman gods
c.	collect taxes from the peasants
d.	bow to the emperor

In his speech, what did Maurice consider the highest calling?

(Circle **the** letter that applies.)

a.	The will of the emperor.
b.	The uprising of the peasants.
c.	The oath to God.
d.	The safety of his homeland.

Radical Soldiers, Continued

Writing

> Write about the characteristics or traits that made Maurice and his Theban soldier martyrs. Try to include traits that are different from Papus and Iulianus and Jon Hus.

The heading on this page calls the Thebans' *radical soldiers*.

> Look the word *radical* up in your dictionary.

> Jot down the meaning that you think applies to Maurice and the Theban soldiers.

> As your last paragraph, write whether you consider the Thebans radical.

> Be sure to support you answer with examples from the story.

**Remember, save your writing on Maurice and
the Theban legion to use later in this chapter.**

A Little Martyr?

Norway becoming a Christian nation

Norwegians converted to Christianity around the tenth century CE. At the time, there were still many folk in the country, living in isolated places, who continued to hold on to the pagan beliefs about Thor, Odin, and Freya – the ancient Norse gods and goddesses. You will read about a young Christian who meets some of these pagans in this next folktale.

A Different Kind of Person

Jon Hus, Papus and Lulianus, and Maurice and his legionnaires – all – were dealing with powerful authorities in their struggle. The little figure in this tragedy was not a soldier or religious leader, but was still a martyr in her own way.

You will read two versions of this story.

> Keep track of the similarities and differences as you read each ballad.

Continued on next page

A Little Martyr?, Continued

"Torgjus' Daughters"
Written down by Sophus Bugge
Told by Signe Napper Skafså, Mo, Telemark, Norway

Torgjus had two little daughters
Long into the morn [morning] they slept
While the sun shone so holy.

Torjus went to the girls' room,
he woke Kari, so proud,
"Get up, Kari," said he, "Get dressed.
"The folk in church are waiting for you."

"Tell the folk," Kari said, …
"Don't wait a bit on me.
"Tell those church folk: I'm coming later"

Kari put on her small dress
sown in golden thread
with a blue skirt. ...

Kari went to the brook,
to comb her golden hair.
She bound her hair with a red-gold band ….

Kari put her blue cape over her shoulders
Then she took the path to the moor.
Then it happened on that moor:
She came upon two bandits.

"Hey," said the first bandit, "are you not a daughter of the Virgin
or are you a daughter of Torjus of the Island,
the sweet maid [young girl] promised to Bendik?"

"I am not Maria maid," she replied.
"I am Torgjus of Island's little girl!"

"How would you like ," said the second, "to be a bandit's wife,
or would you rather die here?"
"I will not be a bandit's wife," said Kari.
"I would rather lose my life."

A Little Martyr?, Continued

Version I
(continued)

Then Kari was laid on a chopping block
And they chopped off her golden lock [hair]
So white, as blood ran Kari's blood;
High candlelight after her blood …

From: http://www.dokpro.uio.no/ballader/tekster_html/b/b021_001.html
[BIN: 1087] Torgjus-døtrane Oppskrift 1857 av Sophus Bugge etter Signe
Napper, Skafså, Mo, Telemark.

(Translated by David Garnett)

Mini-exercise   Complete the study tables. Follow the directions in each table.

Kari was the daughter of _____ .

(Circle **all the letters** that apply.)

a.	the Pope
b.	Torgjus
c.	Thord
d.	Papus

We know Kari was a Christian because she _____ .

(Circle **all the letters** that apply.)

a.	ate only bread on Fridays
b.	was on her way to church
c.	prayed every morning
d.	was humble

Read the
second version

As you read the next version of "Togjus' Daughter," look for
similarities and differences between this version and the one you have
just finished.

Continued on next page

A Little Martyr?, Continued

"Torgjus' Daughters"
Written down by Sophus Bugge

Told by Ingebjørg Kivle & Åste Haugjen of Seljord, Telemark

Kari threw her over shoulders her cape so blue
She set out on the road to the woods on the moor ...
But the sun, it shone so holy,

When she came on to the wild moor,
She met two ruffians on the wild moor,
So said one ruffian:

"Become my wife or die on the moor here."

"I will not be a ruffian's wife,
I would rather die on the wild moor," answered Kari. ...

Then they grabbed Kari by her golden lock [hair]
to take her to the chopping block.

List three differences between this version about Kari and the earlier one:
    1.

    2.

    3.

Continued on next page

A Little Martyr?, Continued

Version II
(continued)

Then they led her [there, to the chopping block]
So far Kari's blood ran
three holy lights shone after her.

Kari, she found herself in heaven, both tired and faint. ...
at the Virgin's red-gold throne,

Kari, she went down on her bare knee, saying-
"My good Lord, forgive the ruffians."

And God replied, "No, Kari, don't pray for those two;
rather pray for your father and mother.

"Your father and mother will come to heaven,
but the two ruffians, you won't ever see them."

> From:
>> http://www.dokpro.uio.no/ballader/tekster_html/b/b021_0
>> 01.html [BIN: 1092] Torgjus-døtrane oppskrift 1874 av
>> Sophus Bugge etter Ingebjørg Kivle og Åst Haugjen,
>> Seljord, Telemark.

(Translated by David Garnett)

Mini-exercise

Complete the study tables. Follow the directions in each table. Use

➤ **Kari I** for Kari in the first version you read.

➤ **Kari II** for Kari in the second version.

Continued on next page

A Little Martyr?, Continued

Looking at the two Kari's, who was richer? Explain.

(Write your answer below.)

Which of the two Kari's was more humble or had more humility? Explain.

(Write your answer below.)

Use a Compare and Contrast organizer with the Kari's

A New Look   The thinking organizer on the next page is a little different from the earlier **Compare and Contrast** organizer that you used with the houses of worship in chapter I. As you look at the organizer, read about how to use it.

Compare

Write a sentence or two about how
the two Kari's are alike or similar.

1.	
2.	
3.	

Contrast

Attribute or Trait	Version I Kari	Version II Kari

Explanation of Contrast

➢ Before we explain the **Contrast** section of this organizer, let's learn a little about attributes or traits (They are the same for any organizer.)

➢ Attributes or traits are especially important when you contrast two things or try to figure out what makes two items different.

➢ Notice the first column under **Contrast**: It says **Attribute or Trait.**

Look at the next section: It gives details and examples of attributes and traits.

Attribute or Trait: Examples

Definition

Look back at **Contrast** of the organizer on the previous page. The first column is very important. It is labeled **Attribute or Trait.** What does this mean?

> **When you contrast any items, you must make sure that you find differences about the same trait or characteristic.**

Let's look at a couple of examples, which follow.

Good Example

You are looking at two soccer balls. You like the colors of the first – red and black -- better than the colors of the second – orange and green.

You have a valid contrast because you are contrasting the soccer balls on the same axis or trait or attribute: **COLOR.**

Poor Example

Two girls are looking at a couple of handbags.

- The first bag has a large carrying strap.

- The second bag has specially dyed cloth.

- Both handbags have patterns and color.

The girls try to talk about the difference (they try to contrast the bags) between the two bags using the carrying strap and the dyed cloth. The carrying strap and the dyed cloth are two different traits or attributes. They are not common to the two bags:

- One bag has one attribute, the carrying strap.
- The other bag has a different attribute, dyed cloth.

So the girls can't show a good contrast or difference between the two bags using these attributes because both purses don't have these two attributes in common. To contrast the two bags, the girls have to use a common trait, such as color, or patterning, which the two bags both have.

Continued on next page

Attribute or Trait: Examples, Continued

Importance of Attribute/Trait

A difference has to come from something that is common to the two items you are contrasting. If the contrast is not based on a common attribute or trait, it is not a valid contrast and will make no sense.

As you can see, you have to figure out the attribute or trait that is common to the things you are contrasting. This axis, attribute or trait:

- Is the baseline for your contrast.
- Guides you in what to look for in order to contrast the two items.
- Is a general feature of the two items.
- Helps you sort the details of the items so that you can find the contrasts.

Mini-Exercise

To help you understand axis, attribute, and trait, do the exercise that follows.
- ➢ Read each study table.
- ➢ Follow the instructions and complete each part of the exercise.

Two butchers are contrasting Argentina chorizo with polish sausage. Chorizo is deep red and speckled. Polish sausage is smooth and pink. Mr. Tim Butcher says that chorizo is extremely hot. That's why he prefers it to polish sausage. Mr. Jan Butcher says that chorizo is not hot enough. Polish sausage is just right though.

(Check **any** statement below that applies.)

	This is a valid contrast. The axis or trait is the spiciness of the sausages.
	This is not a valid contrast. There is no common trait that the butchers are contrasting. To make this a good contrast, the butchers should compare the sausage on _____
	This is a valid contrast because the butchers are contrasting the sausage on the trait of the softness of the sausage.
	Another trait that the butchers might have used to contrast the two types of sausage is their color. This would have been a valid contrast too.

Continued on next page

79

Attribute or Trait: **Examples,** Continued

Think of an apple and a pumpkin. List all the different attributes or traits or characteristics you can contrast an apple and a pumpkin on, to show how different they are. We have started you with the first one.

(Write the traits below.)

i.	The **size** (a trait) of an apple and a pumpkin are different.
ii.	
iii.	
iv.	
v.	
vi.	
vii.	
viii.	

Use an organizer with the Two Kari's

➢ Now, look at the **Compare and Contrast** organizer that follows. Use it to compare and contrast the two versions of "Togjus' Daughters," i.e., the two Kari's.

➢ For **Compare**: Write about both Kari's in the same sentence as you are discussing their likenesses or similarities.

➢ For **Contrast**: Write the attribute in the **Attribute/Trait** column, then check which Kari showed that attribute or trait

Remember, if Kari I shows a trait;
***Kari II* can't show it and vice versa!**

Compare and Contrast the Two Kari's

Compare and Contrast for "Torgjus' Daughters"

Compare
Write a sentence by each number about how
the two Kari's are alike or similar.

1.	
2.	
3.	
4.	
5.	
6.	
7.	
8.	

Contrast

Attribute or Trait	Kari I	*Kari II*
Was rich	**x**	
Was humble		*X*

Continued on next page

Compare and Contrast the Two Kari's, Continued

Writing

Now write about the two Kari's.

- Use **Kari I** for Kari in the first version.
- Use *Kari II* for Kari in the second version.

> - **In the first paragraph, write about the similarities or likenesses between the two versions.**

> - **In the second and following paragraphs, write about the differences or contrasts between the two versions.**

- Use the attributes you list in the **Attribute or Trait** column of the organizer in your topic sentence about a difference.
- Then support the topic sentence with specific examples from each of the versions.

You should have about 4-5 paragraphs on the differences.

> - **In the final paragraph, discuss how you think Kari was a martyr.** Support your answer.

> **Remember, save your writing on "Togjus' Daughters." You will use it later in this chapter.**

Tips on Writing about Comparison and Contrast

Paragraph I

To help you write about the similarities and the differences between the two Kari's, we have included some detailed guidance on writing the paragraphs about the two folk ballads

Introduction

Sentence 1: Write about what you are comparing and contrasting:

> - Name the ballads which are the sources for your comparison and contrast.

> - Name the two objects that you are comparing and contrasting, in this case the two Kari's.

Sentence 2: Write a sentence about Kari I, in this case explaining a little about what happened to her. Follow up with a little detail about Kari II.

Next Sentence: This sentence emphasizes that there are both similarities and differences between the two works.

Continued on next page

Tips on Writing about Comparison and Contrast, Continued

Paragraph II

Compare: Explain the Similarities between the to things

Go back and look at your organizer:
- ➤ Choose three or four similarities or likenesses between the two Kari's.
- ➤ Try to choose the more important similarities.

Now begin writing paragraph II.

Sentence 1: This is a topic sentence that states there are similarities between the two Kari's.

Sentences 2: Talk about one of their similarities: Write about the one that you think is really important!

Sentence 3: Next write about another important similarity.

Sentence 4: Follow sentence 3 with an example of how the two things you are comparing meet the similarity in sentence 3.

Sentences 5: State a third similarity you chose.

Sentence 6: Follow sentence 5 with an example from the organizer of how the two things you are comparing meet the similarity.

Sentences 7: Write the most important similarity.

Sentence 8: Follow sentence 7 with an example of how the two things share this common trait or similarity.

Continue this style of writing if you want to add more similarities.

Paragraph III

Explain the differences between the two Kari's

Sentence 1: This is a transition sentence between the two paragraphs. It should connect the last sentences of paragraph II to the topic of this paragraph. For example, "*Although Kari I and Kari II have similarities, they also have differences.*"

Sentences 2 & 3: Write a sentence using one attribute or trait from **Contrast** in the organizer. Follow sentence 2 with an example of how each of the Kari's is different in regard to the trait. (You may also write additional sentences giving specific examples.)

Continued on next page

Tips on Writing about Comparison and Contrast, Continued

Paragraph III (continued)	**Explain the differences between the two Kari's,** Continued
	Sentences 4 and 5: Write a sentence using the next most important contrasting trait or attribute from the organizer. Follow sentence four with an example of how each of the Kari's is different in this regard. (You may also write additional sentences giving specific examples.)
	Sentences 6 and 7: Write a sentence using the most important trait or attribute from **Contrast** in the organizer. Then tell the reader how each Kari is different in this regard. (You may also write additional sentences giving specific examples.)

Paragraph IV	**Conclusion or Closure**
	➢ Here you restate that there were similarities and differences between the two Kari's.
	➢ You restate what you originally said in the first paragraph, but in different words.

Paragraph V	**Martyr Trait**
	In this final paragraph, write about the martyr traits that the Kari's exhibited. These should not be the same at those you wrote for the earlier "martyrs."
	Be sure to check all your writing for punctuation, spelling and grammar. Most important, check that all the parts fit together!

Another Martyr?

What to do	As you read the story-telling poem called "The Musician's Tale: The Saga of King Olaf" by the American poet, Henry Wadsworth Longfellow, keep track of the small events or incidents in the poem. These are what Longfellow used to build the plot of the poem. You may want to jot down each incident.
	One of these incidents is the most important one in the plot, called the literary climax or high point. You will learn about the literary climax and the anti-climax later in this chapter.

Continued on next page

Another Martyr?, Continued

Look at King Olaf and his rival Iron-Beard

Now take a look at this famous Norwegian king and his struggle to get his people to convert to Christianity. As you read this narrative poem, pay attention to the following:

- The attitude and character traits of King Olaf Tryggvason.
- The attitude and character traits of Iron-Beard.
- What King Olaf and Iron Beard wanted.
- The struggle between the two.
- The results of the struggle.

As you read this narrative poem, think about King Olaf Tryggvason -- was he a martyr? Maybe, he wasn't like Pappus and Lulianus, Jon Hus, or little Kari, but he did something very important for religion in his native land, Norway. See if he doesn't add another trait to you idea about a martyr.

The vocabulary that follows should help with unfamiliar words.

Vocabulary for Olaf Tryggvason

Drontheim = Trondheim, a city on the northwestern coast of present-day Norway

Hus-Ting = a gathering of warriors and farmers for making decisions

confront = about to attack

summons = call

churl = rough, nasty guy

Hammer of Thor = The Norse pagan god Thor had a hammer for making thunder.

cumbersome = awkward

Odin = king of the Norse pagan gods

gore = bloody and torn body parts

smote = hit hard

Read about King Olaf

"The Musician's Tale: The Saga of King Olaf"
Henry Wadsworth Longfellow

Olaf the King, one summer morn,
Blew a blast on his bugle-horn,
Sending his signal through the land of Drontheim.

And to the Hus-Ting held at Mere   *Olaf the king calls all the warriors to a meeting.*
Gathered the farmers far and near,
With their war weapons ready to confront him.

Ploughing under the morning star,
Old Iron-Beard in Yriar   *How did Iron-Beard behave?*
Heard the summons, chuckling with a low laugh.

He wiped the sweat-drops from his brow,
Unharnessed his horses from the plough,
And clattering came on horseback to King Olaf.

He was the churliest of the churls;
Little he cared for kings or earls;   *Iron Beard's character*
Bitter as home-brewed ale were his foaming passions.

Hodden-gray was the garb he wore,
And by the Hammer of Thor he swore;
He hated the narrow town, and all its fashions [he liked the country, hated the city.].

But he loved the freedom of his farm,   *What did Iron-Beard like?*
His ale at night, by the fireside warm,
Gudrun his daughter, with her flaxen tresses [long blond hair].
He loved his horses and his herds,
The smell of the earth, and the song of birds,
His well-filled barns, his brook with its water-cresses.

Huge and cumbersome was his frame;   *How did Iron-Beard look?*
His beard, from which he took his name,
Frosty and fierce, like that of Hymer the Giant [frost giant].

Before you continue, write your answer to the question below:

Name two old Norse pagan figures used to describe Iron-Beard.

1. _____   2. _____

Continued on next page

Read about King Olaf, Continued

So at the Hus-Ting he appeared,
The farmer of Yriar, Iron-Beard,
On horseback, in an attitude defiant.

And to King Olaf he cried aloud,
Out of the middle of the crowd,
That tossed about him like a stormy ocean:

"Such sacrifices shalt thou bring;   *What did Iron-Beard want Olaf to do?*
To Odin and to Thor, O King,
As other kings have done in their devotion!"

King Olaf answered: "I command
This land to be a Christian land;   *What did King Olaf want to happen?*
Here is my Bishop who the folk baptizes!

"But if you ask me to restore
Your sacrifices, stained with gore ,
Then will I offer human sacrifices!   *What will Olaf do if the folk won't become Christian?*

… Then to their Temple strode he in,
And loud behind him heard the din [noise]
Of his men-at-arms and the peasants fiercely fighting.

There in the Temple, carved in wood,
The image of great Odin stood,
And other gods, with Thor supreme among them.

King Olaf smote them with the blade   *What did King Olaf do in the pagan temple?*
Of his huge war-axe, gold inlaid,
And downward shattered to the pavement flung them.

Think about: What kind of sacrifice did Iron-Beard demand of King Olaf?

What sacrifice was King Olaf going to make if the farmers would
not become Christians? Who do you think would be the "human
sacrifices"?

Continued on next page

Read about King Olaf, Continued

At the same moment rose … outside,
From the contending crowd, a shout,
A mingled sound of triumph and of wailing.

And there upon the trampled plain
The farmer Iron-Beard lay slain,   *What happened to Iron-Beard?*
Midway between the assailed [his own men] and the assailing [King Olaf's soldiers].

King Olaf from the doorway spoke.
"Choose ye between two things, my folk,   *What choice does King Olaf give the people?*
To be baptized or … to go to the slaughter!"

And seeing Iron-Beard stark and dead,
The people with a murmur said,
"O King, baptize us with thy holy water."

So all the Drontheim land became
A Christian land in name and fame,
In the old gods no more believing and trusting.

And as a blood-atonement, soon
King Olaf wed the fair Gudrun;   *What happened to Iron-Beard's daughter?*
And thus in peace ended the Drontheim Hus-Ting!"

Adapted from: http://www.hwlongfellow.org/poems_poem.php?pid=2028. This
tale is from *Tales of Wayside Inn*, 1863. Not in copyright.

Answer the following question:

Why did the people asked to be baptized?

(Write your answer below)

What to do   You are going to find the literary climax or high point in the narrative
poem about Olaf Tryggvason. Look at the discussion of literary climax
that follows. Think about the poem as you read about literary climax.

Use a timeline to help you find the literary climax

Definition

As you read this poem, notice a couple of important points:

- How the suspense builds.
- What the high point or turning point is in the narrative.
- What the low point is.

The definitions below will help you understand what to do:

- **LITERARY CLIMAX** is the high point in a work. It may be the point when a hero succeeds or fails. Everything before the high point leads up to it. Everything after the high point drops off and moves toward the end of the narrative or story.

- **ANTICLIMAX** is the drop-off after the climax. It is a lower point. The anticlimax usually results from the climax.

You will explore how Longfellow uses climax and anticlimax in the poem. Now reread the poem, keeping literary climax and anticlimax in mind.

What to do

You will use the **FLOW CHART/TIME LINE** that follows to help you figure out the climax and anticlimax in Longfellow's "The Musician's Tale: The Saga of King Olaf." Read **Tips** below before you fill out the time line.

Tips

Look at the **FLOW CHART/TIME LINE** that follows.

- ➢ In *Column A* – fill in the main events in the plot of the poem in order.

- ➢ In **Column B** – fill in how people, including King Olaf and/or Iron-Beard reacted.

We have filled in parts of the table. You complete it.

FLOW CHART/TIME LINE for "The Saga of King Olaf"

	Column A *What happens in the poem: action or event*	Column B How people reacted or what they did
1.	*King Olaf blows his horn.*	Farmers gather to meet Olaf. They were angry at him.
2.		
3.		
4.	*Iron-Beard shouts defiantly at King Olaf.*	He wants King Olaf to worship and sacrifice to the pagan gods.
5.	*King Olaf replies to Iron-Beard.*	He demands Iron-Beard become Christian.
6.		
7.	*King Olaf sees the images of the pagan gods in the temple.*	
8.		
9.		
10.	*People see Iron-Beard is slain.*	The people ask to be baptized. All Drontheim becomes Christian.
11.	*King Olaf "pays for" Iron-Beard's death.*	

Summarize the literary climax

Writing

Now, using your completed timeline,

- ➤ Decide what incident or event is the literary climax in the poem.
- ➤ Then decide what incident or event is the anticlimax.
- ➤ Write about which is the literary climax and which is the anticlimax. Be sure to use examples from the poem to support your topic sentences.

- ➤ In the final paragraph, write how you think King Olaf was a martyr. What traits did he have – different from the traits of the "martyrs" you read about earlier. Remember, use examples from the poem to support your decision.

**Remember to save your writing on King Olaf.
You will use it later in this chapter.**

Write your own definition of *martyr*

Look at the martyrs in this chapter.

To help you write your idea of what a martyr is, you will use the concept table that follows. Before you start to fill out the table, read **Tips** below.

Tips

➤ Refer back to the writing you did about each earlier martyr. For each, you discussed some important martyr trait(s). These should help you complete the table on the next page.

Looking at the **Martyr Table** on the next page, the name of each "martyr" has been listed under *Name*.

➤ Think of **the** trait that makes each person a martyr and list it under **Trait,** beside that person's name.
➤ Then for **the** trait you listed for a person, write the best example from the story about that person under **Example from tale**.

Finally, if one of the other persons showed this trait, list him/her under **Others who exhibited the same trait**.

Remember, use a different trait for each person!

We have done one of the people. You complete the table.

Write your own definition of *martyr*, Continued

Martyr Table

Name	Trait	Example from tale	Others who exhibited the same trait
Jon Hus			
Pappus and Lulianus			
Maurice			
Kari			
King Olaf	WARRIOR	His men had a battle in which Iron-Beard, a pagan, was killed.	

Continued on next page

Write your own definition of *martyr*, Continued

How to organize

Using the table you completed on the previous page and each of the tales, write your own concept or definition of a martyr.

- ➤ Start with an introduction about martyrs in general.
- ➤ Then describe the trait and the person who most showed that trait in a paragraph.
- ➤ Support the trait with the example for the person.
- ➤ Add any other people who also showed the trait.

This would be one paragraph.

- ➤ You should continue with the other traits and persons, putting each in a separate paragraph.
- ➤ You need a final summary that pulls the traits together so that you give a good idea of how your martyr looks and behaves.

You should have a paragraph for each trait and a final summary paragraph.

Chapter IV
What the divine has touched

Introduction and Overview

Definition

Look back at the story about Solomon and Asmodeus in **Chapter II.** Do you remember the *shamir* in the folk tale? It is a holy instrument that plays an important part in the story.

In this chapter you will explore what the divine has touched. In and of themselves, the objects you will read about are not necessarily holy, but in the context or meaning of a particular religion, God, Allah, Jehovah, or "the divine" has touched the object and given it a special, holy meaning. You can probably name a few of them.

- Some of these are holy relics or implements, that is, people in the folk tale can actually touch these blessed things.

- Others cannot be touched by humans. They are intangible, but are still blessed and made holy.

**What to do:
Learning
Objectives**

Define the idea of "what the divine has touched" in folktales by:

➢ Exploring selections to find what the divine has touched.

➢ Using new graphic organizers.

➢ Defining personification.

**Companion
Guide**

This workbook is a companion to a teacher guide and curriculum source: *"Snipp snapp snute, så er eventyret ute"* – *Folklore Reader and Critical Thinking Workbook*, which has additional critical thinking materials and reading selections.

Continued on next page

Introduction and Overview, Continued

**Content:
Selections**

The selections in this chapter include:

- An excerpt from Stephen Hawker's 'The Quest of the Sangraal."
- An excerpt from Robert de Boron's version of the Holy Grail legend.

- "Psalm 104" from the Old Testament
- "Hymn to Aten" (by Akhenaton)

- Jacobs' Ladder from Luke 11:34-36
- A Selection about St. John Climacus' Ladder
- "St. Perpetua's Dream" from Tertullian, 5. Appendix

Two Relics from the Time of Jesus

A Poem

As an introduction to "What the divine has touched," read the poem that follows; you will learn about two holy relics associated with Jesus.

Continued on next page

Two Relics from the Time of Jesus, Continued

Vocabulary　　Use the vocabulary below to help you with unfamiliar words.

Sangraal = Another name for the Holy Grail

awful = worthy of wonder

Pascha = Greek name for Easter

Jesu = Jesus'

ruddy = red colored

tawny = light brown or brownish orange color

ethereal = heavenly

ever and anon = forever and ever

this dear land = England

Aron's rod = A magic "wand" or rod, one belonging to Moses and the other, to Aaron. They were to divide the waters of the Red Sea and to cause water to gush from a rock in the desert. When Aaron cast his rod before pharaoh and his magicians, the rod became a serpent.

82. From 'The Quest of the Sangraal'
Robert Stephen Hawker

Then came Joseph of Arimathea,
Bearing that awful vase, the Sangraal!
The vessel of the Pascha, [on] Thursday night:
The same cup, wherein the faithful with holy wine
Heard God ...

Then Arimathea ... gathered blessèd drops
That sadly fell from Jesu side,
Those ruddy [red] dews from the great Tree of Life:
Sweet Lord! what treasures! like the priceless gems,
Hid in the tawny casket of a king—
A ransom for an army, one by one.

Continued on next page

Two Relics from the Time of Jesus, Continued

All things were strange and rare: the Sangraal
As though it clung to some ethereal chain,
Brought down high heaven to earth to Arimathea,
Who lived long centuries and prophesied.

A girded pilgrim was St. Joseph ever and anon:
Cross-staff [staff in the form of a cross] in hand, and folded at his side was
The mystic marvel of the feast of blood!
Once in old time, he stood in this dear land,
Enthralled: for lo! a sign! his staff in the ground
Took root, branched out , and bloomed, like Aaron's rod;
Then came the shrine, the cell: therefore, he dwelt,
The keeper of the Sangraal, at Avalon!

From: Nicholson & Lee, eds. The Oxford Book of English Mystical Verse.
1917. Not in copyright. At: http://www.bartleby.com/236/82.html

---

Mini-exercise   Complete the study tables below. Follow the directions in each table.

The two holy relics in this poem are _____

(Circle **the appropriate letter/s.**)

a.	a plate from the Last Supper and a cloak of Jesus.
b.	a basket belonging to Mary and a sandal from Jesus.
c.	a cup called the Sangraal and a cross-staff.
d.	a cloth used to wash Jesus' brow and a bowl to hold water.

The person carrying the Sangraal was _____

(Circle **only one letter**.)

a.	the Roman Catholic pope.
b.	Joseph of Arimathea.
c.	Joseph, the husband of Mary.
d.	Apostle Paul.

Continued on the next page

Joseph of Arimathea travelled from _____ to _____

(Circle **only one letter**.)

a.	Jerusalem to Italy.
b.	Nazareth to Cairo.
c.	Jerusalem to England.
d.	Nazareth to Spain.

Joseph d'Arimathie and the Holy Grail

Another Version

Now read this version of Joseph d'Arimathie and the Holy Grail (San Graal). Note the similarities and differences between the two tales.

The ... Holy Grail is [also called] the Cup of Christ or Joseph d' Arimathie's Cup. This is the vessel that Joseph d'Arimathie used to catch the blood and sweat of ... Jesus after he was taken down from the Cross. It is the same cup that Jesus passed among his disciples as part of the first communion during the Last Supper.

According to Robert de Boron's version of the Holy Grail legend, Joseph d'Arimathie was incarcerated [imprisoned] in a Jerusalem prison, where the Jewish authorities had placed him after the body of Jesus suspiciously disappeared from its tomb.

One day while in his cell, Joseph found the Cup suddenly ... placed at his feet by God, who then proceeded to explain "the secrets of the Grail," which are the secrets of the Eucharist ... .

Joseph was kept alive for many years by food and drink that would spontaneously appear in the Cup . Joseph d'Arimathie continued to remain nourished by the chalice [cup] until Jerusalem was conquered by the Roman Emperor Vespasian. ... Then Joseph was released from prison.

Before you continue with the tale, answer the question below:

List three differences between this story about Joseph and the earlier one:

1.

2.

3.

Continued on next page

Joseph d'Arimathie and the Holy Grail, Continued

Fearing re-imprisonment and renewed torture from both the Jews and Romans, Joseph d'Arimathie escaped to the desert with his family, where both he and they were continually sustained by the sacred Cup.

Joseph d'Arimathie died soon after going into the desert, but not before placing the Cup into the care of his brother-in-law, Bron, whose inner guidance subsequently led him across the sea, north to Glastonbury, Britain, where he was told to … [leave] the Grail.

Adapted from: *A Multitude of Holy Grails – Part I*
By Mark Amaru Pinkham © 2005
At: http://www.universalhealingnetwork.com/articles/holygrail1.htm

Compare and Contrast: *Joseph of Arimathea and the Sangraal* with *Joseph d'Arimathie and the Holy Grail*

An Old Friend

Look at the **Compare and Contrast** thinking organizer that follows. It should be familiar to you. You used it to compare and contrast the two Kari's.

- If you have to, go back to the chapter about martyrs and review how to use the organizer.

- Then compare and contrast the "two" Joseph's.

Compare and Contrast for the two Joseph's

Compare

Write a sentence by each number about how
the two Joseph's are alike or similar.

1.	Both Joseph's received the cup.
2.	
3.	
4.	
5.	
6.	
7.	
8.	

Contrast

Attribute or Trait	Joseph of Arimathea (Graal)	Joseph d'Arimathie (Grail)
Had a brother-in-law named Bron		X
Went to England	X	

Continued on next page

Compare and Contrast: *Joseph of Arimathea and the Sangraal*
with *Joseph d'Arimathie and the Holy Grail,* Continued

Writing   Now write about the similarities and differences between the folktale of
                   the Sangraal and the story about the holy grail.

Untouchable?

What has the   The Sangraal was a religious object which people could touch and feel.
divine touched?   In the next section, the divine touches something which is not so easy to
                      get your hands on. It has become extremely important in all religions.

                      Since there are many approaches to this object that the divine has
                      touched, you will spend time working with it. Instead of naming what
                      the divine has touched this time, you will read two short examples about
                      this "object."

> ➢ As you read this first selection, see if you can figure out what the
> author is singing about.

> ➢ Pay attention to the *words marked like this.*

Hebrew Psalm   Read Psalm 104 from the Old Testament. The author is talking
                      about God (Jehovah), but how does he describe Jehovah? This is one of
                      the few instances in the Bible where God is described exactly like this.

Psalm 104

Praise the Lord, O my soul.
O Lord my God, you are very great;
you are clothed with splendor and majesty.

He [the Lord] wraps himself in light as with a garment;
he stretches out the heavens like a tent.

The moon marks off the seasons,
and the sun knows when to go down.

You [Lord] bring darkness, it becomes night,
and all the beasts of the forest prowl[roam about].

The lions roar for their prey
and seek their food from God.

Continued on the next page

Untouchable?, Continued

The sun rises, and they [the lions] steal away;
they return and lie down in their dens.

Then man goes out to his work,
to his labor until evening.

How many are your works, O LORD!
In wisdom you made them all;
the earth is full of your creatures.

When you send your Spirit,
They [the Lord's works] are created,
and you renew the face of the earth.

May the glory of the Lord endure forever;
may the Lord rejoice in his works.

I will sing to the Lord all my life;
I will sing praise to my God as long as I live.

May my meditation be pleasing to Him,
as I rejoice in the LORD.

Mini- exercise   Do the study tables below. Follow the directions in each table.

The main subject of this poem is _____

(Circle **only one** letter.)

a.	a famous martyr.
b.	the prophet Muhammad.
c.	God or Jehovah.
d.	a bishop.

Continued on next page

Untouchable?, Continued

List four things the psalmist says that the Lord does:

(Write your list below.)

1.	
2.	
3.	
4.	

In the last six lines of the poem, "May the glory of the Lord endure forever … rejoice in the LORD." **the psalmist** _____

(Circle **only one** letter.)

a.	tells a story about God.
b.	talks about prophets loving Jehovah.
c.	tells about conquering Satan.
d.	sings praises to the Lord.

Relationships: Whole to Parts

IMPORTANT!   In this section, you are going to figure out the organization of Psalm 104. This means dividing the psalm into its main parts or subjects. To do this you will used a **Whole and Parts** organizer.

First, let's do some preparation. On the next page, Psalm 104 has been duplicated. This time we have put lines in places where we think a new part or subject starts in the poem.

> Look carefully at the psalm with the lines inserted.
> Try to figure out why we put the line where we did. What might be the main subject of each group between the inserted lines?
> Then think of a good name or topic for each section.

Continued on next page

Relationships: Whole to Parts, Continued

Psalm 104

Praise the Lord, O my soul.   **Section I**
O Lord my God, you are very great;
you are clothed with splendor and majesty.

He [the Lord] wraps himself in light as with a garment;
he stretches out the heavens like a tent.

The moon marks off the seasons,   **Section II**
and the sun knows when to go down.

You [Lord] bring darkness, it becomes night,
and all the beasts of the forest prowl[roam about].

The lions roar for their prey
and seek their food from God.
The sun rises, and they [the lions] steal away;
they return and lie down in their dens.

Then man goes out to his work,
to his labor until evening.

How many are your works, O LORD!   **Section III**
In wisdom you made them all;
the earth is full of your creatures.

When you send your Spirit,
They [the Lord's works] are created,
and you renew the face of the earth.

May the glory of the Lord endure forever;   **Section IV**
may the Lord rejoice in his works.

I will sing to the Lord all my life;
I will sing praise to my God as long as I live.

May my meditation be pleasing to Him,
as I rejoice in the LORD.

As we divided the psalm into its parts or subject areas, notice how we
numbered each part. Look at the next page to see how we filled out the
Whole to Parts thinking organizer. Be sure to read the tips in each
part of the organizer.

Whole to Parts Thinking Organizer: Psalm 104

First, write the whole:

> **The Whole is: Psalm 104**

Content	Section I	Section II	Section III	Section IV
Subject/Topic of Section	*Splendor of the Lord in the sky*	*Moon, sun, darkness and light*	*Works and creations of the Lord*	*Praise and rejoicing in God*
Possible Title of Section	*God is light*	*Lord's control of time*	*Lord – the source of all*	*Ending Hymn*

Explanation of the Table

Content refers to what the psalmist sings about in each section of the Psalm. Under **Content**, there are two important headings:

> **Subject/Topic of Section**, which is a summary of important things in each section of the poem.

> **Possible Title of Section**, which is the topic that you will use in the main or topic sentence when you write about each section.

Writing

Now that you have seen how to use this thinking organizer:

Use the organizer and Psalm 104 to write about the different topics the psalmist sings about.

- The possible title of each section might be part of the topic sentence for each paragraph.
- Then the subject/topic of each section might be examples or part of a supporting sentence for the topic sentence. You can also go back to the psalm and get examples there.
- You should have four-five paragraphs about the different parts of Psalm 104.

Another Hymn: You find the parts

A Little Background

This hymn was written by an ancient Egyptian pharaoh around 1390 BCE. This pharaoh, named Akhenaton, was a monotheist [he believed in only one god.] While he lived, he and his family led Egypt in a religion that worshiped only one god, called Aten. With Akhenaton's passing, The ancient Egyptians reverted back to polytheism [the worship of many gods].

- ➢ Read Akhenaton's "Hymn to Aten."
- ➢ Pay attention to the different topics or subject areas.

"Hymn to Aten"
Akhenaton

When thou settest [set or go down] in the western horizon of heaven
The world is in darkness like the dead.
Every lion comes forth from his den,
The serpents they sting. Darkness reigns.

Bright is the earth when thou [Aten] riseth in the horizon. . .
The two lands [Egypt consisted of two kingdoms] are in daily festival,
Awake and standing upon their feet. . .
Then in all the world they [humans] do their work.

… O thou sole [the only] god, whose power no other possesses.
Thou didst create the earth according to thy desire, being alone:
Man, all cattle, large and small;
All that are upon the earth.

Adapted from: http://www.touregypt.net/hymntoaten.htm

Whole to Part

Fill in the **Whole to Part** thinking organizer using the "Hymn to Aten."

- ➢ First divide the hymn into sections.
- ➢ Then fill in the different parts of the table.

We had made the table for four sections.

Whole to Parts for "Hymn to Aten"

┌───┐
│ The Whole is: │
└───┘

Content	Section I	Section II	Section III	Section IV
Subject/Topic of Section				
Possible Title / Topic Sentence				

Writing   Using your completed organizer and the "Hymn to Aten," write about the different parts of the poem.

Wood and Ladders?

Introduction

Wood is something that the divine has touched in many ways and many times. Remember the quotation from Psalm 23 "Thy rod and thy staff ..." Both the rod and the staff were made from wood.

In this section, you will explore other ways the divine has touched wood.

Really?

Ladders, can you believe it? They have formed an integral part of "r"eligious folklore traditions. Let's see how ladders are treated, first in the Old Testament.

A Ladder from the Old Testament

The Old Testament has the first reference to a ladder. Read the passage below from "Genesis."

Genesis 28:11-19
(New International Version)

[11] When he [Jacob] reached a certain place, he stopped for the night because the sun had set. Taking one of the stones there, he put it under his head and lay down to sleep. [12] He had a dream in which he saw a ladder resting on the earth, with its top reaching to heaven, and the angels of God were ascending and descending on it. [13] There above it stood the LORD, and he said: "I am the LORD, the God of your father Abraham and the God of Isaac.

Think about: What do you think are the basic elements or parts of the story about Jacob's ladder? A ladder is definitely one element. Can you see other elements or parts?

Continued on next page

Wood and Ladders?, Continued

The Original Ladder

This one short incident in the Old Testament has given rise to lots of ladders in those religions that followed after Judaism. As you read the next couple of selections, pay attention to such changes as place, time, size, and importance of Jacob's reinterpreted ladder.

Thirty Rungs to the Divine

Saint John Climacus' Ladder

"He was surnamed "of the Ladder" (Climacus) because he wrote an immortal work, the *Ladder of Divine Ascent*. In this work, we see how, by means of thirty steps, a Christian gradually [goes up the thirty steps] to the heights of … spiritual perfection. We see how one virtue [on each step] leads to … [the next virtue above it]. A Christian climbing each step rises higher and higher and finally … gets to that … [top] where … the crown of the virtues, which is called "Christian love" is. … Saint John wrote his immortal work especially for the monastics [monks], but his ladder was always a favorite reading for anyone … [eager] to live piously. …

"When we throw a stone up, it ascends [goes up] until the moment when the propelling force ceases to be effective. So long as this force acts, the stone travels higher and higher … , overcoming the force of the earth's gravity. But when this [upward] force is spent [finished] … , then, as you know, the stone does not remain … [up] in the air. Immediately, it begins to fall, and the further it falls the greater the speed of its fall – all this according to the physical laws of … gravity.

"So it is also in the spiritual life. As a … [person] gradually [goes up], the force of … [the spirit] lifts him higher. … Now, if the Christian … ascending this ladder of spiritual perfection by his struggles and ascetic [meditative and spiritual efforts], ceases [stops climbing] … , his soul will not remain, [moving upward]; but, like the stone, it will fall to the earth. More and more quickly … it will drop. If the person ... does not come to his senses, he will … fall lower and lower.

"Let us remember this. Saint John Climacus has described the ladder of spiritual ascent; then let us not forget that each [of us] must … [climb the ladder]. The great ascetics [monks and hermits] ascended [climbed up] like swiftly flying eagles, [but] we scarcely ascend at all. … Let us not forget that, unless we … use our efforts … [to] correct ourselves and our lives, we shall cease [stop] our ascent, and, most assuredly, we shall begin to fall. …"

From: "Sermon on the Sunday of St. John of the Ladder" by Metropolitan Philaret of the Russian Orthodox faith. At: http://www.stjohnthebaptist.org.au/articles/ladder.html

Continued on next page

Thirty Rungs to the Divine, Continued

Mini-exercise   Do the study tables below. Follow the directions in each table.

A person's struggle to climb up the thirty rungs of the ladder is compared to _____   (Circle **only one letter**.)

a.	raindrops freezing to hail and falling to earth.
b.	a feather floating around in the wind.
c.	gravity's effect on a stone tossed into the air.
d.	little birds flying out from their nest.

The purpose of climbing the thirty rungs of the ladder

is to _____   (Circle **all the letters** that apply.)

a.	reach the top and become an angel.
b.	reach spiritual perfection.
c.	understand God's divinity.
d.	find all the people in your past.

Describe below in your own words the difference between the way great ascetics climb and the way everyday folks climb the ladder.

A Saint's Ladder

St. Perpetua   As you read about St. Perpetua's dream of a ladder, compare it to the two previous ladders. Notice the changes and additions or embellishments to Jacob's ladder.

St. Perpetua's Dream
(from Tertullian, 5. Appendix)

St. Perpetua … dreamed of a golden ladder of marvelous height, reaching up even to heaven, and very narrow, so that persons could only ascend it one by one; and on the sides of the ladder was fixed every kind of iron weapon. These ... were swords, lances, hooks, daggers, so that if anyone went up carelessly, or not looking upwards, he would be torn to pieces and his flesh would cleave [stick to] to the iron weapons. … Under the ladder was crouching a dragon of wonderful size, who lay in wait for those who ascended. [The dragon] frightened them from [going up].

Saturus went up first; … [he had] … freely [become a martyr] … . He attained [got to] the top of the ladder and turned towards me and said to me, "Perpetua, I am waiting for you; but be careful that the dragon doesn't … bite you."

And I [Perpetua] said, "In the name of the Lord … , he shall not hurt me." And from under the ladder itself, as if in fear of me, [the dragon] slowly lifted up his head. As I trod [stepped] on the first step, I trod on his head. … I then went up, and I saw an immense … garden. In … the garden, a white-haired man [was] sitting in the dress of a shepherd, milking sheep. … Standing around were many thousand white-robed ones.

… The [white-haired man] raised his head, … looked at me, and said to me, "Thou are welcome, daughter." Then … he called me. From the cheese as he was milking, he gave me … a little cake, and I received it with folded hands. Then I ate it, and all who stood around said, "Amen."

At the sound of their voices, I … [woke up], still tasting a sweetness which I cannot describe. And I immediately related this to my brother. …"

Adapted from: http://users.netnitco.net/~legend01/ladder.htm

Mini-exercise   Do the tables on the next page. Follow the directions in each table.

Continued on next page

112

A Saint's Ladder, Continued

List below four differences between St. Perpetua's ladder and Jacob's ladder.

1.	
2.	
3.	
4.	

The difference between what St. Perpetua attained or reached on her ladder and what an ascetic reached by means of St. John Climacus' ladder is _____

(Circle **all the letters** that apply.)

a.	The ascetic reached paradise; St. Perpetua came to a barnyard.
b.	The ascetic reached the source of God; St. Perpetua found the source of the gold on her ladder.
c.	The ascetic reached spiritual perfection while St. Perpetua reached paradise.
d.	The ascetic saw a man all dressed in white while St. Perpetua saw a shining sword to cut off the dragon's head.

What do you think the cheese might represent?   (Write your answer below.)

Compare ladders

Continued on next page

What to do

You are going to compare Jacob's ladder, the oldest version, with the two later versions. You will:

> ➢ Make the Old Testament excerpt the base line for your comparison.
> ➢ Show what additions or changes the later ladders made to the original.
> ➢ Finally write about the changes and/or additions that were made to the original Old Testament ladder.

Basic Elements of the Old Testament Version

Go back to the section about Jacob's ladder. Read about his ladder again. The basic parts or elements of the Old Testament ladder are among other things: Jacob and the ladder.

Now list all the elements of this Old Testament story. We have listed a couple of them.

1. Jacob, who is dreaming, on earth.

2.

3. Angels going up and down the ladder.

4.

Another Organizer

The **Sort** organizer on the next page will help you see the changes and additions to the original Jacob's ladder:

> ➢ In the first column **Jacob's Ladder**, list the original elements of the Old Testament Jacob's ladder from your list above.
> ➢ In the second column, **Changes or Additions in St. John's Ladder**, list any change or addition that occurred in St. John Climacus' ladder.
> ➢ In the next column **Changes or Additions in St. Perpetua**, list any change/addition to the basic elements in St. Perpetua's ladder.

We have started the table. You complete it.

**Remember, your guide in sorting is
the original Old Testament ladder.**

Continued on next page

Sort for the Ladders

Jacob's Ladder: Original Elements	Changes or Additions in St. John's Ladder	Changes or Additions in St. Perpetua
Jacob is dreaming.	St. John wrote about his ladder.	St. Perpetua dreams.
Content of the Dream		
A Ladder from earth to heaven	A Ladder of 30 rungs	A ladder of gold.
		Iron weapons on the side of the ladder
Jacob remains on earth.		St. Perpetua climbs her ladder.
	A way to spiritual perfection	

Continued on next page

Contrast the ladders

Writing   Write about the changes and/or additions to Jacob's original ladder in John Climacus' ladder and St. Perpetua's ladder. Read **Tips** below to help you in your writing.

Tips   As mentioned earlier, the baseline for your writing is the original elements or parts of Jacob's Old Testament ladder.

➢ Each paragraph of your writing should begin with one of these elements from Jacob's ladder.

➢ Refer back to each of the selections and to your **Sort** table.

In writing, you might:

➢ Make the topic sentence of each paragraph include information about the original element from Jacob's ladder.

➢ Use the changes in John Climacus' ladder and St. Perpetua's ladder in supporting sentences for each topic sentence.

➢ Add in, at the right place, elements in the other two selections that don't occur in Jacob's ladder.

➢ In the final paragraph, discuss which two of the three excerpts are more similar. Explain.

Chapter V
Dragons

Introduction and Overview

Definition

It might seem strange to learn about dragons in "r"eligious folktales, but dragons played a prevalent role in many early folktales.

You know about dragons: There is the dragon that Bilbo Baggins met in Tolkien's *Hobbit*. C. S. Lewis wrote about dragons in his Narnia series. Do you remember the dragon in the story of St. Perpetua? There are many kinds of dragons in 21st century video games and television shows. So dragons should not be any stranger to you.

**What to do:
Learning
Objectives**

In this chapter your will:

➤ Explore various "r"eligious folktales about dragons.

➤ Contrast the dragon folktales.

➤ Decide about how a dragon folktale developed and changed into different versions

**Companion
Guide**

This workbook is a companion to another critical thinking source: *"Snipp snapp snute, så er eventyret ute" – Folklore Reader and Critical Thinking Workbook* which has additional critical thinking materials and reading selections.

Continued on next page

Introduction and Overview, Continued

Chapter Components

A text or group of texts that you will read. Most of the writing and other work you do require you to read and refer to these text resource(s).
Any of a number of activities or exercises which you need to complete. These activities may include:

- Vocabulary exercises.
- Questions to answer.
- Study tables to complete
- Thinking organizers (graphic or picture diagrams) to fill out.
- Written work to plan, organize, and write.

All these activities should help you to read and understand the texts or to write about them. You may have to complete a project, which requires limited research.

Content: Selections

The selections in this chapter include the following "r"eligious folktales about:

- St. David and the dragon.

- St. Martha and the dragon called Tarasque.

Three versions of St. George and the dragon from:
- Palestine
- England
- Norway

You will also use the tale about St. Perpetua from **Chapter IV**.

A Georgian Saint and His Dragon

A Little Background

St. David is famous in Georgia. Georgia is a country in the Caucasus. The country was once a part of the old Soviet Union, but is now independent.

Georgians are trying very intensely to modernize. They speak Georgian, a language not related to most other languages. They belong to the Orthodox faith like the Greeks and the Russians. There are also Muslims in the country.

Continued on next page

A Georgian Saint and His Dragon, Continued

What to do   As you read about St. David look for the following points in this story:

- The kind of dragon St. David was involved with – what it looked like and how it behaved.

- How St. David reacted to the dragon, for example, did he fight in anger with the dragon?

- How the dragon was subdued or conquered.

Keep these points in mind as you will need to look at some of the other dragons in this chapter in the same way.

St. David and the Dragon

St. David of Georgia had always wanted to be a hermit and live alone … . So he left to live in desolate and waterless places. He chose to live outside in the wilderness, and for this reason his desert abode [home] is called Garesja. He took with him one disciple, Brother Lucian.

When St. David and Brother Lucian had arrived in this uninhabited and waterless place, they found a cave in a crag and settled down in it. Whenever it became sultry [hot and dry] or rained, the two of them stayed in the cave. For food, they collected roots and grass. As it was spring, ...plenty of food was to be found.

Then the hot and dry summer came; the meadows withered and burned up. Suddenly three deer, followed by their fawns came by and stood like sheep before St. David and Lucian. St. David said, "Brother Lucian, take a dish and milk these deer." Lucian got up and milked them. When the dish was full, he took it to St. David, who made the sign of the cross and turned the milk into cheese, which the two of them then ate. After that, the deer came every day, except fast days, and brought their fawns with them.

Before you continue with the folktale, answer the question below:

What happened to the deer milk when St. David prayed over it?
(Write your answer below.)

Continued on next page

119

A Georgian Saint and His Dragon, Continued

… Underneath, close by the cave where the saints resided [lived] was another cave, in which was a large and fearful dragon with bloodshot eyes and a horn growing out of his forehead, … with a great mane on his neck. One day, the deer were going by the entrance to the cave when the dragon attacked them, … seized a fawn and swallowed it. The other terrified deer ran to St. David and trembled. When Lucian saw them shivering with fright, he said to St. David, "Father, these deer have come flying to us and are shaking with terror, and they have left one of their fawns behind."

So the hermit St. David went out with his staff in his hand. When he had reached the cave which the deer had passed by, he saw the dragon and said,

> **"Evil dragon, why have you harmed our deer, which God has given us for milk and cheese? Now leave here, and go far away into the desert. If you do not obey me, then by the power of our Lord, I will rip open your stomach with my staff and turn you into food for mice."**

The dragon answered,

> **"Do not be angry, O servant of God! If you want me to leave here, lead me up to the top of that mountain and promise that you will not take your eyes off me until I have reached the river which flows on the south side of the hills, because I am afraid of thunderbolts and cannot endure them."**

St. David gave his promise. Then the dragon set out with St. David, who was reciting a psalm as they went. When Lucian saw this, he was afraid, and fell on his face and lay as if dead. St. David led the dragon up as far as the top of the mountain, and the dragon began to scramble up to the peak. When the dragon had left the plain, St. David set off back towards his cave keeping his eye on the dragon. But the angel of the Lord spoke from behind him and said, "St. David!" So the saint looked round, and as he turned, the dragon was struck by a thunderbolt and completely burnt up.

When St. David saw this, he was very sorry and said, "O Lord, why did You kill this dragon which put its trust in me?"

Continued on next page

A Georgian Saint and His Dragon, Continued

Then the angel of the Lord said to him,

> "Why are you sorry? If the dragon had entered the river, he would have passed out into the sea. Then eating the fish there, he would have grown enormous, and would have overturned many ships in the ocean and destroyed many creatures in the seas. So do not grieve because the Lord has shown His mercy in this way, but go to your cave. Your disciple Lucian has fallen on his face and is lying terror-stricken from fear of the dragon. Stretch out your hand, and raise him up, … strengthen and fortify [give support] him."

The angel then departed. St. David found Lucian quaking [shivering] with fear, lying on the earth. He stretched out his hand and raised Lucian up and said, "Brother Lucian, why were you frightened of a worm, which God has shriveled up with fire in an instant? Now do not be afraid, for the might of God is with us. God's grace protects all." So Lucian was cheered by the hermit's words.

Adapted from: http://www.angelfire.com/ga/Georgian/david.html and from http://en.wikipedia.org/wiki/Thirteen_Syrian_Fathers

Martha from the Bible

From Jesus' time

Martha is famous in the Holy Bible. Look at the excerpt below so that you have an idea who she was.

Luke 10:38-42
(New International Version)

At the Home of Martha and Mary:

38As Jesus and his disciples were on their way, he came to a village where a woman named Martha opened her home to him. 39She had a sister called Mary, who sat at the Lord's feet listening to what he said. 40But Martha was distracted by all the preparations that had to be made. She came to him and asked, "Lord, don't you care that my sister has left me to do the work by myself? Tell her to help me!"

41"Martha, Martha," the Lord answered, "you are worried and upset about many things, 42but only one thing is needed. Mary has chosen what is better, and it will not be taken away from her."

Continued on next page

Martha from the Bible, Continued

What to do   Now read the selection about Martha, later called St. Martha, and the dragon Tarasque. Remember to look for the following in this folktale:

- The kind of dragon St. Martha was involved with – what it looked like and how it behaved.

- How St. Martha reacted to the dragon, for example, did she fight in anger with the dragon, called Tarasque.

- How Tarasque was subdued or conquered.

- What the final outcome for Tarasque was.

Continued on next page

Martha from the Bible, Continued

"La Tarasque"

A long time ago, a huge monster emerged from the sea and chose the Rhone River in France as its new home, [near the town of Nerluc]. The beast was a dragoness [female dragon], half land mammal and half fish. She outsized [was larger than] twelve elephants, had teeth like swords and … skin like iron. Her father was the water dragon Leviathan, her mother the giant snake Onachus, and her name was Tarasque. Wherever the beast appeared, she brought terror and destruction. All animals fled … . She destroyed houses, and her breath was flames. Many heroes tried to kill her and perished. ...

Seven … years went by. The Tarasque had destroyed all bridges and devoured everyone who wanted to cross the river. At last the inhabitants of the troubled area tried to lure the dragoness into a trap. Near the town of Avignon, there was a deep swamp. Whoever went there [sank into the swamp] and was lost. So they bound animals to trees near the trail leading to the swamp. The beast followed this line of [animals]. But when she approached the trap, she turned around and fled back to the river: The swamp belonged to... the devil, and being a creature of the devil herself, the Tarasque was warned and [escaped the trap].

Again seven years passed. Then one day, Saint Martha happened to visit the area. When she heard of the beast, she went out to catch it - barefooted, in her white dress, with no other weapon than a jar of holy water. The dragoness came out to devour [the saint], but was quelled [controlled] solely by the power of the cross and the holy water.

St. Martha led the beast to the town, where it was killed. The citizens erected a new church in honor of St. Martha, and the town changed its name to Tarascon.

Before continuing, write your answer to the question below:

Go back and reread about St. Perpetua (Do you remember the section about ladders?) and her dragon: **Now list three differences between St. Perpetua's dragon and La Tarasque.**

1.

2.

3.

Contrast: Remember!

Tips on Contrast

You are going to contrast the three dragons: St. Perpetua's from **Chapter IV**, St. David's, and La Tarasque. Before you begin, Let's review how to contrast or show differences.

Importance of Trait or Action

In the case of the dragons, you have to contrast or show a difference on a general trait or action, such as how the dragons were subdued or conquered. Another trait you could contrast them on is each dragon's appearance.

Common: Very Important in Contrast

A difference has to come from something that is **common to the items you are contrasting**. If the contrast is not based on a common trait or action of the dragons, it is not a valid contrast and will make no sense.

As you can see, you have to figure out the general traits and actions that are common to the three dragons. A trait or action:

- Is the baseline for you contrast.
- Guides you in what to look for to contrast in the dragons.
- Is a general feature of the three dragons.
- Helps you sort the details of the items so that you can find the contrasts.

Do the exercise on the next page to help you understand trait and action when contrasting.

Continued on next page

Contrast: Remember!, Continued

Think of a country cottage and a palace. List all the different traits you can contrast these two items on, to show how different they are. The traits should be general and common to a cottage and palace. We have started you with a couple. See if you can complete the table below.

(Write the traits below.)

i.	The **sizes** of a country cottage and a palace are different.
ii.	The **setting or location** of each is different.
iii.	
iv.	
v.	
vi.	
vii.	
viii.	
ix.	

Contrast St. Perpetua's dragon, St. David's dragon, and La Tarasque

How to use the matrix

You will use a **Contrast Matrix** to explore the differences among the three dragons. Read the information below to help you with the matrix.

1. First think of :

   - Some attributes about the dragon, for example how he looked and what things he did.

   - The ways that the saint who "conquered" the dragon reacted or got involved with the dragon.

   - What happened to the dragon, for example, how he was subdued or how he was killed.

   - You can get these general traits from the stories.

2. Now list these general traits and actions in the first column of the matrix called **Traits and Actions**.

3. Next check under each saint if his or her dragon had that particular trait or action.

If you do this, you will have a good idea of the differences among the three dragons. We have started the matrix; you complete it.

Continued on next page

Matrix for the Three Saints' Dragons

Traits and Actions	St. Perpetua's Dragon	St. David's Dragon	La Tarasque
Talked with the saint		X	
Was eventually killed		X	X

Writing   Using your completed matrix, write about **the differences** among St. Perpetua's dragon, St. David's dragon, and La Tarasque. Read **Tips** to help you.

Continued on next page

Contrast St. Perpetua's dragon, St. David's dragon, and La Tarasque, Continued

Tips

> ➤ Choose the attributes and actions that are important and show the greatest contrast among the three folktales.

> ➤ Use each general attribute and action you listed in the first column of the matrix in your topic sentence for a paragraph.

> ➤ Supporting sentences and examples should come from each tale.

> ➤ You should have 3-5 paragraphs that discuss the differences.

A Famous Knight and his Dragon

World Famous Knight

St. George is a very famous knight. He is known throughout the religious world. Muslims and Christians both have legends about him. Read about St. George's life on the next page.

Continued on next page

A Famous Knight and his Dragon, Continued

It is likely that Saint George was born to a Christian noble family in Lydda, Palestine, between about 275 CE and 285 CE, and he died in Nicomedia. His father was a Roman army official from Cappadocia, and his mother was from Palestine. They were both Christians and from noble families, so George was raised with Christian beliefs. They decided to call him Georgius (Latin) or Geōrgios (Greek), meaning "worker of the land." At the age of 14, George lost his father; a few years later, George's mother died.

Then George decided to go to Nicomedia, the imperial city of that time. He became a soldier in Emperor Diocletian's imperial army. Diocletian, who was a pagan, welcomed him with open arms, as he had known George's father, who was one of his finest soldiers. By his late 20s, George was promoted to the rank of tribune and was stationed as an imperial guard of the emperor at Nicomedia.

In 302 CE, Diocletian issued an edict that every Christian soldier in the army should be arrested if he did not offer a sacrifice to the pagan gods. George objected and approached the emperor. Diocletian was upset, not wanting to lose his best tribune. George loudly renounced the Emperor's edict. In front of his fellow soldiers and tribunes, he said he was a Christian.

Diocletian attempted to convert George back to paganism, even offering gifts of land, money and slaves if he made a sacrifice to the pagan gods. The Emperor made many offers, but George never accepted.

Recognizing the futility of his efforts, Diocletian had no choice: He had to have George executed. Before the execution, George gave his wealth to the poor and prepared himself. After various torture sessions, including laceration on a wheel of swords in which George was resuscitated three times, George's head was cut off before Nicomedia's city wall, on April 23, 303 CE. A witness to the saint's suffering convinced Empress Alexandra and Athanasius, a pagan priest, to become Christians as well. They were then executed too. The saint's body was returned to Lydda for burial, where Christians soon came to honor him as a martyr.

Adapted from: Wikipedia, the free encyclopedia
At: http://en.wikipedia.org/wiki/Saint_George

So, where is St. George's dragon? That is a piece of folklore that grew up through the years after his death. The folktale eventually became a world-wide legend, spreading to many countries as you will see.

Continued on next page

A Famous Knight and his Dragon, Continued

What to do

This is the Muslim version of St. George, who is called *Mar Jiryis* in Arabic.

- ➢ Read this folktale about Mar Jiryis.
- ➢ Look for the simple basic elements that make up this story.

Mar Jiryis and the Dragon
(from Palestine)

There was once a great city that depended for its water supply on a [spring] … [outside] its walls. Then a great dragon … took possession of the … [spring] and refused to allow anyone to take water from the spring. [The dragon said,] "You can draw water from the … [spring] whenever you bring a … youth or maiden to the … [spring] for me to devour."

The people tried again and again to destroy the monster, but though the best warriors of the city went … [out] against the dragon, its breath was so pestilential [like a plague] that people used to drop … dead before they came within bow-shot of the dragon.

The terrorized inhabitants had to sacrifice their [children] … or die of thirst. At last, all the youth of the place had perished, except the king's daughter. So great was the distress of their subjects from thirst that her heart-broken parents could no longer withhold her. … [from sacrifice to the dragon.]

[With great wailing and weeping of the people,] the king's daughter went out towards the spring, where the dragon lay waiting [for] her. But just as the noisome [very annoying] monster was going to leap on her, Mar Jiryis appeared … on a fine white steed. [With his] spear in hand, … Mar Jiryis rode full tilt [right straight] at the dragon He struck [the spear] … [square] between the eyes and laid [the dragon] dead.

The king, out of gratitude for this … [unexpected] succour [help], gave Mar Jiryis his daughter and half of his kingdom,"

Adapted from: http://www.sacred-texts.com/asia/flhl/flhl12.htm and from:
http://www.archive.org/stream/folkloreholylan00unkngoog/folkloreholylan00unkngoog_djvu.txt Not in copyright.

Mini-exercise

Do the **Elements** table that follows.

Continued on next page

A Famous Knight and his Dragon, Continued

Elements for Mar Jiryis

Which of the following are simple, basic elements that must be in the folktale about Mar Jiryis (St. George)?

(Circle **all the letters** that apply.)

a.	A golden sword.
b.	A dragon that terrorizes the people.
c.	A queen who loves her daughter.
d.	A king who doesn't want to sacrifice his daughter.
e.	The problem with the well.
f.	A king's daughter, who is willing to sacrifice herself to the dragon.
g.	Mar Jiryis, who saves the king's daughter.
h.	The marriage of the king's daughter and Mar Jiryis.

The knight moves away

**Same Knight/
Different
Place?**

Look at this story about St. George. This time the setting is in England. See if you can figure out the changes to this story because it moved to England.

St. George and the Dragon
(from England)

Once upon a time, long ago, there was a good king, … [who had] a little daughter, Sabra. … He loved Sabra better than his fields, ...his gold, or anything which he had. … Little Sabra was as fair as a lily, as sweet as a rose, and as kind and true [as a perfect gem].

Then a terrible thing happened to the king: Down from the mountains and straight through … the king's city came a ravening [very hungry] dragon. It was black and horrible to look at, with eyes like two red coals and a mouth that breathed fire and [fumes]. Its jaws were wide and full of sharp teeth; its claws were sharp, and it was as tall and huge as a forest tree.

Through the king's fields, it raged and ...tore up … the harvest of barley, rye and wheat. It killed the cattle and uprooted the grape vines. … Nor did it stop with the fields. It lay in wait by the river bank in the tall reeds [for people]. … No one in the whole kingdom was brave enough to kill it.

Continued on next page

The knight moves away,

The king sent his nobles to beg the dragon to leave, but ... it would not. ... This is the message the dragon sent to the king: Each morning the king must send one of the fairest little girls in the whole kingdom and ... [tie] her to an old oak tree by ... the river; then the dragon [would] devour [the little girl] at his pleasure. Unless the king did this, the farmers would not be allowed to go back to the fields, and there would be no food in the land.

There was great grief in the kingdom. Each mother held her little girl more closely so that she should not be the first one to go. There was great hunger, for no one could plant or harvest the crops. But little Sabra still laughed and sang as joyously as ever.

"Father, dear," Sabra cried, "let me be the first little girl to go. I know if the dragon has your little princess, he will ask for no other child. I will go in their place ... ."

Then the people came crowding to the palace gates, begging the king not to send Sabra, for they all loved her like their own little ones, but still Sabra said: "I will go to the dragon."

A wise councilor of the court told the king: "If we set a pigeon free, and it flies to the east, we must put Sabra out as a sacrifice for the monster. If the pigeon flies west, we are saved, and she won't have to be sacrifice."

Before continuing with this story, write your answer to the question below:

> **Think about England: where it is located; the kind of climate in the country; the homes and buildings the English built at the time of this folktale; the kind of ruler the English have.**

> **Now write a brief paragraph about the "English" things that were possibly added to the original folktale about Mar Jiryis to make this an English "r"eligious folktale.**

Continued on next page

The knight moves away, Continued

So they took a … pigeon from her nest and set her free in the courtyard. She spread her white wings and circled about in the air, and then flew straight to the east! Poor, sweet little Sabra! They carried her out to the river bank and fastened her to the oak tree where the dragon could find her – so that she might save the other little girls. Then they went sorrowfully back to the city … .

But the pigeon flew on and on, through field and forest, until she came to a brave knight riding through the woods. The knight [and his good horse were both] …tired, … for they had been in a far country and had fought many brave battles. He had stopped to rest under a tree [and to allow] … his horse … to drink at the spring. … As he rested, the mother pigeon flew straight to his shoulder and began cooing softly in his ear. "'I wonder what she means," said the knight to himself, as the pigeon flew off a little way and then returned, cooing. At last he jumped on his horse and followed [where] ... the pigeon led.

Straight through field and forest, the pigeon flew until she brought the knight to the place where the Princess Sabra was fastened to the oak tree. The dragon close by ready [was ready] to devour her.

The dragon's breathing was so hot that it burned the knight, and the smoke from its nostrils blinded the knight's eyes, but he was brave and strong. He made a huge ball of the sticky pitch [like liquid tar] from the pine tree; he thrust the end of his spear through it, and he rode straight toward the dragon's angry jaws. The dragon reached out its sharp claws for the knight. Then the knight hurled the ball of pitch down the dragon's throat. The dragon … couldn't open ... its mouth. The knight killed the dragon with his spear and unfastened Sabra [from the oak tree]. He lifted her onto his saddle and carried her home to her father … .

Before you continue with this folktale, answer the question below.

List three important differences between this tale and the earlier one from Palestine.

1.

2.

3.

Continued on next page

The knight moves away, Continued

Oh, there was great rejoicing in the kingdom! The people crowded around the knight … and strewed [threw down] flowers all the way for the knight to ride over. The old king held little Sabra close to his heart, and she put her arms about his neck and kissed him. The king said the knight should be called St. George. Then he gave St. George a wonderful gold cross … .

It was … many years ago that St. George killed the dragon, but … the people in England still remember him, … Only … [an] English soldier who is the bravest may wear a tiny cross like St. George's. St. George is the patron saint of England.

Mini-exercise   Complete the study tables. Follow the directions in each table.

Embellishments in St. George of England

An embellishment is an addition or an added detail. You can probably think of two or three embellishments in the St. George of England tale – embellishments that might have been added to the folktale about Mir Jiryis.

List below five embellishments that are found in the St. George story from England; which of them might have been added to the tale about Mar Jiryis?

1.	
2.	
3.	
4.	
5.	

The knight moves farther away

St. Georg og Draken
(from Telemark, Norway)

There lies a dragon [called *en drake* in Norwegian] by Babylon palace. He would tear the palace down. He won't have as food other than [only] the flesh of a Christian man. He would have to drink nothing other than pure virgin's blood.

The king in the palace ... went with sad mind to his daughter and said, "You will [go] out to the dragon today – I'll never forget it."

Then his daughter ... put on her silken gown, put the golden crown on her head. Nor did she forget God's holy name, the highest in the world. So she went out from the castle with a little knife in her hand.

Then along came a little young fellow who pleased her so much it hurt. "Listen here, listen here, o handsome young fellow, do you want to keep your life or would you risk your life for me and fight the dragon?"

Then they stood a while. The time wasn't long, for the dragon came up from the sea, and the young fellow ran at him. The [little princess'] knife he thrust into the dragon's mouth and the sword he drove into its heart. So can each and every one of us say, in truth, it caused the dragon great pain.

"Hear now, hear now, you, young beautiful woman, tie him up with your belt. Then lead him back to the castle, and I myself will follow," said the young man. So the two of them led the dragon forth to the castle. Then all the walls burst. There had died so many heathens from the dragon's foul breath.

"Listen, father sweet," said the girl, what will you give this young man because he has risked his life for me and fought the dragon?"

"I give him silver and gold and my kingdom too. And I will give you to him. You must be his wife."

And Georg replied: **"No, keep your silver and gold**
And also your daughter so bold
To heaven have I dedicated myself
God grant me this to hold."

Translated from: http://www.dokpro.uio.no/ballader/tekster_html/b/b010_001.html [BIN: 1024] St. Georg og draken. Oppskrift 1857 av Sophus Bugge etter Gunvor Folleigdalen, Vrådal, Kviteseid, Telemark.   (Translated by David Garnett)

The knight moves farther away, Continued

Mini-exercise   Complete the study tables. Follow the directions in each table.

In general, the Telemark folktale about Georg is _____

(Circle all the letters **that apply.)**

a.	More complex than the English folktale about St. George.
b.	Has fewer people than the folktale about Mar Jiryis.
c.	Has more conversation than the English folktale about St. George.
d.	Is simpler than the story about Mar Jiryis.

If we hadn't labeled the story "from Telemark, Norway," how could you tell from the story itself that it comes from that country?

What are some of the clues? Think about the clothing of the king's daughter; her attitude toward the "little, young fellow." Some things that were part of the two other folktales are missing from this one about Georg.

(Write your answer below.)

Find the changes from Mar Jiryis to Georg of Norway

Variants of the Same Tale?

Although you can't be sure, it is possible that the folktale about Mar Jiryis is the earliest of the three you have just read. This might be because:

- The setting for Mar Jiryis is nearest to where St. George originally came from, the Middle East.

- All the essential, basic elements in Mar Jiryis come up in the tale from England and the one from Norway.

- Both the tale from England and the one from Norway had some changes that are unique or special to the countries where the tales were told.

In the matrix that follows, you will sort out the possible changes or embellishments to the original Mar Jiryis folktale.

Continued on next page

Change Matrix for Mar Jiryis, St. George, and Georg of Norway

Traits and Actions	*Mar Jiryis*	St. George	*Georg*
Had a daughter named Sabra		X	
Used a ball of tar to fight the dragon		X	
Killed the dragon with a sword			*X*
Killed the dragon with a spear	*X*	X	
Released a pigeon		X	

Summarize the changes in the folktale

Writing   Write about the changes, either additions to or subtractions from, the Mar Jiryis folktale. Read **Tips** below to help you with your writing.

Tips   You may want to include some of these topics in the paragraphs of your writing:

- Changes to the people in the story.

- Changes to the dragon and other animals in the tales.

- Differences in clothing.

- Differences in how the knight fought and killed the dragon.

- Incidents or events that were added or changed in the tales.

- The way that each folktale ends.

For Notes

Chapter VI
Transformations

Introduction and Overview

Definition

Remember St. David and the milk from the deer. What happened to the milk when St. David prayed over it? This kind of change is called a transformation in folktale research. You are going to read a number of transformations in "r"eligious folktales.

What to do: Learning Objectives

In this chapter you will learn to:

➢ Define attitude in three versions of an ancient Greek folktale.

➢ Discuss the characteristics of the style of the folktale about Baucis and Philemon by Jonathan Swift.

➢ Explain which two of the three versions of a short folktale are probably closest or most related.

➢ Fill in organizers, such as compare and contrast, sorting etc.

➢ Learn how to build a piece of writing paragraph-by-paragraph.

Companion Guide

This workbook is a companion to a teacher guide and curriculum source: *"Snipp snapp snute, så er eventyret ute"* – *Folklore Reader and Critical Thinking Workbook,* which has additional critical thinking materials and reading selections.

Continued on next page

Introduction and Overview, Continued

Chapter Components

A text or group of texts that you will read. Most of the writing and other work you do require you to read and refer to these text resource(s).

Any of a number of activities or exercises which you need to complete. These activities may include:

- Vocabulary exercises.
- Questions to answer.
- Study tables to complete
- Thinking organizers (graphic or picture diagrams) to fill out.
- Written work to plan, organize, and write.

All these activities should help you to read and understand the texts or to write about them. You may have to complete a project, which requires limited research.

Content

The selections in this chapter include:

- "Baucis and Philemon" by Thomas Bulfinch.
- A folktale about the olive tree from Turkey.
- Jonathan Swift's version -- "Baucis and Philomen."
- Excerpts from Edward Fitzgerald's *The Rubaiyat of Omar Khayyam*.
- "The Little Girl and the Wolf," by James Thurber.

Three little-bird folktales:

- "Gjertrudsfuglen" from Norway.
- A Native American folktale.
- A folktale from Finland.

Kindness rewarded: A Folktale from Ancient Greece

A Greek myth   The original folktale you will read is from Greek mythology. You will read three versions of the tale. As you read, see how each version differs from the others.

"VI. b. Baucis and Philemon"
Thomas Bulfinch

On a certain hill in Phrygia [in modern Turkey] stand a linden tree and an oak, enclosed by a low wall. Not far from the spot is a marsh, formerly good habitable land, but now indented with pools, the home of fen-birds and cormorants.

Once upon a time, Zeus, [leader of the ancient Greek gods] in human shape, visited this country, with his son Hermes (also in human form without his wings). They came in the form of weary travelers to many homes, seeking rest and shelter. They found all closed because it was late and the inhospitable inhabitants would not rouse [get up] themselves to open their doors and receive the two tired men.

At last they came to a … small thatched cottage, where Baucis, a pious old woman, and her husband, Philemon, a couple of many years, received Zeus and Hermes. ... When the two guests crossed the threshold, and bowed their heads to pass under the low door, the old man placed a seat, on which Baucis, bustling and attentive, spread a cloth, and begged them to sit down. Then she raked out the coals from the ashes and kindled up a fire, fed it with leaves and dry bark, and with her weak breath blew it into a flame. She brought split sticks and dry branches, broke them up, and placed them under the small kettle. Her husband collected some herbs in the garden, and she shredded them from the stalks, and prepared them for the pot. Philemon reached down with a forked stick for a flitch [slab] of bacon hanging in the chimney, cut a small piece, and put it in the pot to boil with the herbs, putting away the rest for another time. Then he filled a beech bowl with warm water, so that their guests could wash.

On the bench for the guests was a cushion stuffed with sea-weed; and a cloth, used only for special occasions … was spread over bench. The old lady, in her apron, with trembling hand, set the table. One leg of the table was shorter than the rest, but a piece of slate put under the leg made the table level. When fixed, Baucis rubbed the table down with some sweet-smelling herbs. Upon it, she set some olives, some … berries preserved in vinegar, and added radishes and cheese, with eggs lightly cooked in the ashes. All were served in earthen dishes with an earthenware pitcher and wooden cups … .

Continued on next page

Kindness rewarded: A Folktale from Ancient Greece,
Continued

When all was ready, the stew, smoking hot, was set on the table. Some wine …
was added, and for dessert, apples and wild honey. Of course, there were, above
all, friendly faces and a simple but hearty welcome.

Now while they were all eating, the old folks were astonished to see that as fast as
the wine was poured out, it refilled the pitcher, of its own accord. Struck with
terror, Baucis and Philemon recognized their guests, fell on their knees, and with
clasped hands implored forgiveness for their poor fare [food and drink].

There was an old goose, which they kept as the guardian of their cottage; and they
thought about making this a sacrifice to honor their guests. But the goose, too
nimble, eluded [escaped] them and at last took shelter between the gods
themselves. The gods forbade it to be killed and said: "We are gods. This
inhospitable village shall pay the penalty of its impiety; you alone shall go free
from the chastisement [the punishment]. Leave your house, and come with us to the
top of that mountain over there."

The old couple hurried to obey and, staff in hand, struggled up the steep ascent.
They had just reached the top, when looking below, they saw all the country had
sunk into a lake, only their own house was left standing.

While they gazed with wonder at the sight, their old cottage was changed into a
temple. Columns took the place of the corner posts, the thatch grew yellow and
became a gilded [golden] roof, the floors became marble, the doors were
decorated with carving and ornaments of gold.

Then Zeus said : "Excellent old man, and woman worthy of such a husband,
speak, tell us your wishes; what favor would you ask of us?"

Before you continue, answer the question below.

List five transformations in this folktale:

1.

2.

3.

4.

5.

Continued on next page

Kindness rewarded: A Folktale from Ancient Greece,
Continued

Philemon whispered a few seconds with Baucis. Then he told the gods their wish. "We ask to be priests and guardians of your temple, and since we have lived here all our lives in peace and harmony, we wish that we may die together, at the same moment."

Their prayer was granted. They were the keepers of the temple as long as they lived. When very old, they stood one day before the steps of the temple and were telling the story of the place. Then Baucis saw Philemon begin to put forth leaves, and old Philemon saw Baucis changing in the same way. Next a leafy crown grew from their heads. While exchanging parting words, as long as they could speak -- "Farewell, dear spouse," they said to each together. At the same moment, the bark closed over their mouths. The local shepherd still shows the two trees, standing side by side, made from the two good old people, Baucis and Philemon.

Adapted from: Thomas Bulfinch. *Age of Fable,* Vols. I & II: *Stories of Gods and Heroes,*1913. Not in copyright. At: http://www.bartleby.com/181/062.html

Kindness rewarded: A Version from Turkey

A Later Version   Here is a later version from Turkey. Do you see any differences between the two folktales?

Story about the Olive Tree
(from Turkey)

Once many centuries ago, Zeus, the chief of the ancient Greek gods, heard that there was no goodness left on earth. People behaved very bad. So he decided to find out if what he had heard about man was really true. He changed himself into an old man and went down to earth.

Zeus went around for quite a while, but it seem as though no one cared about him. One day, Zeus knocked on the door of a house where an old couple lived. The woman was called Babkis, and the man, Filomon. They lived in a little lonely house far out in the country. When the old couple saw an old man standing at their door, they asked him in and gave him food and drink. They themselves didn't have very much, but they shared it with the old man. Zeus stayed at the couple's house a couple of days, and as payment for his lodging and food, he helped them on their farm.

Zeus had found what he sought and told Babkis and Filomon about the purpose of his visit. He gave them one wish; it could be anything they wanted. Zeus promised to honor them and fulfill their wish. Babkis and Filomon had no children and had wanted a child all these years, but time had passed and they had become old. Instead, the two of them asked to die together.

Continued on next page

Kindness rewarded: A Version from Turkey, Continued

The years passed. One day Filomon collapsed as he was working the farm. Babkis rushed to him and realized that he was dying. She called on Zeus and said the time had come. Zeus let the pair die together. On the place where they died together, it is said the very first olive tree grew.

Adapted from: http://www.tyrkiahus.eu/web_no/legends.htm

From Folktale to Literature: A Poem

Borrowers   The author of the poem below is Jonathan Swift, who is famous for the story about Gulliver and the Lilliputians in *Gulliver's Travels*.

Swift borrowed the story of Baucis and Philemon from a Roman poet named Ovid, who wrote about the old man and his wife in 17 BCE.

What to do   As you read,

> ➤ Keep track of the changes that Swift made to the original tale.
> ➤ Look at Swift's attitude toward the story and the characters of Baucis and Philemon.

"Baucis And Philomen"
Jonathan Swift

On The Ever-Lamented Loss of the Two Yew- Trees in the Parish Of Chilthorne, Somerset. 1706. Imitated From The Eighth Book Of Ovid.

It happened on a winter night,	*What kind of weather?*
As authors of the legend write.	
Two brother hermits, saints by trade.	*Who are visiting around?*
Taking their tour in ***masquerade*** [in funny disguise].	
Disguised in tatter'd habits [ragged monk clothes], went	
To a small village down in Kent [town in England];	
Where, in the strollers' canting strain,	
They begged from door to door in vain.	*Where does the poem take place?*
Tried every tone [to] pity win;	
But not a soul [person] would let them in.	

Continue on next page

From Folktale to Literature: A Poem, Continued

Our wandering saints, in woeful [poor, miserable] state.
Treated at this ungodly rate.
Having through the [whole] village passed.
To a small cottage came at last
Where dwelt a good old honest yeoman,   *Look up "yeoman" in the dictionary.*
Called Philemon.

He kindly did these saints invite
In his poor hut to pass the night;
And then the hospitable sire [man]
Bid **Goody [Mrs.] Baucis** mend the fire.

Philomen from the chimney took
A flitch [slab] of bacon off the hook,   *What kind of food did the guests get?*
And freely from the fattest side
Cut out large slices to be fried.

Then he stepped aside to fetch them drink,
Filled a large jug up to the brink [edge],
And saw it fairly twice go round;
Yet (what was wonderful) they found
The jug was replenished [refilled] to the top.
As if they never had [drunk] a drop.   *What happened to the drink in the jug?*
The good old couple were amazed,
And often at each other gazed ;
For both were frightened to the heart.
And just began to cry, "What are you?"
Then softly turned aside, to view
Whether the lights were burning blue.

Before you continue with the poem, write your answer below:

Name three English things that Swift has added to the story.

1.

2.

3.

Continued on next page

From Folktale to Literature: A Poem, Continued

The gentle pilgrims, soon aware too,
Told the old couple their calling [who they were] and their errand:
"Good folks, Do not be afraid,
We are but saints," the hermits said;
"No harm shall come to you or yours:
But to that **pack of churlish boors** [raw rednecks, your neighbors].
Not fit to live on Christian ground,
They and their houses shall be drowned;
While you'll see your cottage rise,   *What will happen to the neighbor homes?*
And grow a church before your eyes."   *What will happen to their cottage?*

The saints scarce had spoke, when fair and soft,
Philemon's roof began to mount aloft [up in the air];
Aloft rose every beam and rafter;
The heavy wall climbed slowly after.
The chimney widened, and grew higher   *What happened first?*
Became a steeple with a spire.

The kettle to the top was hoist [lifted up],
And there stood fastened to a joist [beam of wood],
But with the upside down, to show
Its inclination [angle] for below :
In vain; for a superior force
Applied at bottom stops its downward course: *What happened to the kettle?*
Doomed ever in suspense to dwell,
the kettle is no kettle, but a bell.

A wooden jack [a spit for roasting lamb and pork] in the chimney had almost
Lost by disuse the art to roast,
A sudden alteration feels.
Increased by new cogs and wheel; ...
Now hardly moves an inch an hour.
The jack and chimney, near allied.
Had never left each other's side ;
The chimney to a steeple grown,   *What happened to the chimney?*
The jack would not be left alone;
But, up against the steeple reared.
Became a clock, and still adhered. ...   *What happened to the jack?*

From Folktale to Literature: A Poem, Continued

The groaning-chair began to crawl.   *What did the chair become?*
Like a huge snail, along the wall ;
There stuck aloft in public view,
And with small change, to a pulpit grew.

The porringers [a low dish or cup with a handle for soup] that in a row
Hung high, and made a glittering show.
To a less noble substance changed,   *What about the porringers?*
Were now but leather offering buckets ranged.

A bedstead of the antique mode,
Compact of timber many a load,
Such as our ancestors did use.
Was metamorphosed [changed] into pews;   *How about the bed?*

The cottage, by such feats as these,
Grown to a church by just degrees,

The hermits then desired their host
To ask for what he would like most.
Philemon, having paused a while,
Returned them thanks in homely style;
Then said, "My house is grown so fine,
Methinks [I think], I still would call it mine.   *What did Philemon wish for?*
I'm old and would rather live at ease;
Make me the parson [preacher or minister] if you please."

He spoke, and presently he feels   *How was his wish fulfilled?*
His coat falls down to his heels :
He sees, yet hardly can believe,
About each arm a pudding [puffed out] sleeve ;
His waistcoat to a cassock [preacher's black clothes] grew.
And both assumed a sable hue [color] ;
But, being old, continued just
As threadbare, and as full of dust. ...

Before you continue, write your answer to the question below.
Name four funny transformations Swift uses in his poem.

1.

2.

3.

4.
_____

Continued on next page

From Folktale to Literature: A Poem, Continued

Thus having furbished up [spruced up] a parson.
Dame Baucis next they played their farce on.
Instead of homespun coifs [kerchiefs], were seen
Good pinners [little white bonnets] edged with colberteen [lace] ;
Her petticoat [underwear], transformed apace,
Became black satin, fringed with lace.
"Plain Goody" would no longer down,
  She now was called "Madam," in her gown.
Philomen was in great surprise,
And hardly could believe his eyes.
Amazed to see her look so prim,
And she admired as much at him.   *How did Baucis change?*

Thus happy in their change of life.
Were several years this man and wife :
When on a day, which proved their last.
Discoursing over old stories past.
They went by chance, amid their talk.
To the churchyard to take a walk.

When Baucis hastily cried out,   *Did they really die?*
"My dear, I see on your forehead a sprout!" —
"Sprout;" said Philomen, "what's this you tell us?
I hope you don't believe me jealous !
But yet, methinks, I feel it true.
And really your head's budding too —
Nay, — now I cannot move my foot;
It feels as if it were taking root."
Description would but tire my Muse,
In short, they both were turned to yews [trees].

Mini-exercise   Complete the study tables. Follow the directions in each table.

Continued on next page

From Folktale to Literature: A Poem, Continued

How serious do you think Jonathan Swift, the author of the poem, was about the folktale of Philemon and Baucis?

(Circle **all the letters** that apply.)

a.	He is very serious because he sticks close to the original folktale.
b.	He is not serious because he makes up foolish transformations in his poem.
c.	Swift is not serious because he makes fun of Zeus.
d.	Swift is not serious since he makes Baucis and Philemon talk with an English country accent.

Comparing the two other versions to Swift's poem, you might say:

(Circle **the letter** that applies.)

a.	The other two poems make fun of Baucis because he is so old.
b.	Swift alone expresses his "opinion" about the poem in the way he writes it.
c.	The other two folktales are very biased in their telling of the story.
d.	Swift is a commentator on the story.

Look at attitude/tone

Definition

You have probably already noticed the difference between the way the two earlier folktales were told and the way Jonathan Swift wrote his poem about the old man and woman. Swift:

- Uses humor in the poem.
- Creates some funny transformations.
- Makes fun of the old couple.
- Uses comical speech.

All these literary techniques indicate Swift probably had a certain approach or attitude toward the story of Baucis and Philemon. He wasn't going to tell the tale in the same vein or way that the two other folktales had been presented.

A Little about Attitude or Tone

Before you start to explore attitude in Swift's "Baucis and Philemon," let's get a better idea of the definition. To do this, we will look at attitude in a number of short selections.

A Rainy Incident

"It's raining 'cats and dogs," said a friend of mine. "Fine weather for ducks."

On the surface, that sentence **"Fine weather for ducks."** seems to be cheerful about the rain, The sentence seems to say that my friend is really enjoying the rain.

- The attitude or tone conveyed by the word *duck* told me that my friend was actually unhappy about the downpour. He was expressing sarcasm when he said that only a duck could enjoy the rain.

- *Sarcasm* is the way or manner in which my friend showed his unhappiness with the weather. Sarcasm expressed my friend's attitude.

Continued on next page

Look at attitude/tone, Continued

Two attitudes	A blind girl sat on a street corner, with a shawl by her feet. She held up a sign which said: 'I am blind, please help.' There were only a few coins on the shawl.
	A woman passed by. She took a few coins from her purse and dropped them onto the shawl. She then took the sign, turned it over, and wrote some words on the other side. She put the sign back so that everyone who walked by would see the words she had written. Soon there were many coins on the shawl. A lot more people were giving money to the blind girl.
	That afternoon the same woman came to see how things were. The girl recognized her footsteps and asked, "Did you change my sign this morning? What did you write?"
	The woman said, "I said what you said but in a different way."
	What she had written was:
	"Today is a beautiful day and I cannot see it."
	Think about this little incident. Then write a paragraph that answers the questions below.
	Do you think the first sign and the second sign were saying the same thing? What made the difference between the two?

Continued on next page

Look at attitude/tone, Continued

A Little Prig

➢ Look at this example of attitude below.

➢ Pay attention to the words ***bolded and italicized*** like this. These are key words to defining the attitude or tone in this incident.

Mary ***surveyed*** the other girls in the gym. She was congratulating herself for ***snatching*** the position of chief cheerleader without practicing at all, unlike all the other clumsy ***klutzes*** in the class.

Now answer the question below.

The words ***surveyed***, ***snatching***, and ***klutzes*** suggest Mary's _____

(Circle **only** one answer.)

a.	angry attitude.
b.	indifferent attitude.
c.	arrogant or superior attitude.
d.	gentle attitude.

Find attitude in the Baucis and Philemon texts

What to do

Reread the two folktales about Baucis and Philemon, one from ancient Greece and the other from Turkey. The look again at Jonathan Swift's "Baucis and Philemon."

➢ Think about the kind of attitude expressed in each selection.

➢ Fill out the table on the next page before you begin writing.

➢ Read **Tips** first.

Continued on next page

Find attitude in the Baucis and Philemon texts, Continued

Tips

➤ In each box, write a short paragraph about the selection **on the top line of the table.**

- To help you, go back to each selection and concentrate on the word printed *like this*. They may be clues to the attitude in the text.

- You may find that there is no attitude in a particular text. This would mean the text was neutral, without any attitude.

➤ As you write each paragraph, be sure to include an example or two from the selection to support your topic sentence about the attitude in the selection.

Write below your paragraph about attitude in the ancient Greek myth.

Continued on next page

Find attitude in the Baucis and Philemon texts, Continued

Write below your paragraph about attitude in the Turkish tale.

Continued on next page

Find attitude in the Baucis and Philemon texts, Continued

Write below your paragraph about Swift's attitude in his poem.

Continued on next page

Find attitude in the Baucis and Philemon texts, Continued

Writing

➤ Now combine the three paragraphs from the tables on the previous pages into one piece of writing. Try to put transitions between the paragraphs.

➤ You should have at least three paragraphs, one for each selection.

➤ Your fourth paragraph should be your evaluation of which text best expresses an attitude.

What style of writing is Swift's poem?

A Clue

At the beginning of Swift's poem there is a kind of dedication, which reads:

"On The Ever-Lamented Loss of the Two Yew-Trees in the Parish Of Chilthorne, Somerset. 1706. Imitated From The Eighth Book Of Ovid."

This "dedication" tells us two things. Do the study tables below to discover these two important points.

The words "Ever-Lamented Loss" seem to say that

_____   (Circle **all the letters** that apply.)

a.	Swift is going to be very sincere about Baucis and Philemon.
b.	he will make fun of the original Greek myth.
c.	Swift will probably change the plot of the story.
d.	he might make fun of the story of the two old people.

"Imitate" means that _____   (Circle **all the letters** that apply.)

a.	the poem will be an exact copy of the story that Ovid told..
b.	Swift will copy the style of the original myth.
c.	he will produce a comic story, with possible exaggeration..
d.	Swift plans a serious poem about the old folks' devotion..

Continued on next page

What style of writing is Swift's poem?, Continued

Writing   Now write your answer to the question below.

Looking back at the poem, especially the "dedication," and the study tables you have just completed, write about the two important points that Swift was going to use in his poem.

| |
| |
| |
| |
| |
| |
| |
| |
| |
| |
| |
| |
| |
| |

"Imitation"   The key word in the "dedication" is *imitation*. Swift's poem is an imitation of the Greek myth as a Roman author, Ovid, told it. We will look at some other selections to explore this kind of imitation. In each case, you will read the original and then the imitation.

A Spiritual Poem from Persia (Iran) and its Imitators

East meets West

In the 19th century, an American writer named Edward Fitzgerald translated an ancient Persian poem called the *Rubaiyat of Omar Khayyam*.

- The poem in quatrains caught the American public, who went crazy over this spiritual poem by a Muslim poet.

- Below are some quotes from Fitzgerald's original translation. Each is followed by an imitation. As you read, think about what all the imitations have in common.

From the original *Rubaiyat of Omar Khayyam*.

WAKE! For the Sun who scatter'd into flight
The Stars before him from the Field of Night,
Drives Night along with them from Heav'n, and strikes
The Sultan's Turret with a Shaft of Light.

From *The Rubaiyat of a Persian Kitten* by Oliver Herford, 1904. (Not in copyright.)

Wake! For the Golden Cat has put to flight
The Mouse of Darkness with his Paw of Light:
Which means, in Plain and simple every-day
Unoriental Speech---The Dawn is bright.

From the original *Rubaiyat of Omar Khayyam*.

And that inverted Bowl they call the Sky,
Whereunder crawling coop'd we live and die,
Lift not your hand to It for help---for It
As impotently moves as you or I.

From *The Rubaiyat of a Persian Kitten* by Oliver Herford, 1904. (Not in copyright.)

And that Inverted Bowl of Skyblue Delf [a deep blue porcelain made in Holland]
That helpless lies upon the Pantry Shelf---
Lift not your eyes to It for help, for It
Is quite as empty as you are yourself.

From http://www.oldfashionedamericanhumor.com/the-rubaiyat-of-a-persian-kitten.html

---

A Modern "Folktale" Imitation

Little Red Who?

Below is a modern version of a famous folktale. The author of the new version was a 20th century American humorist and writer. See what he did to the original tale, which you will recognize immediately.

"The Little Girl and the Wolf"
James Thurber

One afternoon a big wolf waited in a dark forest for a little girl to come along carrying a basket of food to her grandmother. Finally a little girl did come along and she was carrying a basket of food. "Are you carrying that basket to your grandmother?" asked the wolf. The little girl said yes, she was. So the wolf asked her where her grandmother lived and the little girl told him and he disappeared into the wood.

When the little girl opened the door of her grandmother's house she saw that there was somebody in bed with a nightcap and nightgown on. She had approached no nearer than twenty-five feet from the bed when she saw that it was not her grandmother but the wolf, for even in a nightcap a wolf does not look any more like your grandmother than the Metro-Goldwyn lion looks like Hannah Montana. So the little girl took an automatic [a pistol] out of her basket and shot the wolf dead.

(Moral: It is not so easy to fool little girls nowadays as it used to be.)

Adapted from: http://andromeda.rutgers.edu/~lcrew/quotes/picnicba.html
And from: http://unrealnature.wordpress.com/2008/03/30/the-little-girl-and-the-wolf/

Now complete the study table below.

Looking at the original excerpts from *The Rubaiyat of Omar Khayyam* and the original folktale about Little Red Riding Hood and the imitations, the main trait that the imitations have in common is

_____ .

(Circle **all the letters** that apply.)

a.	they are much shorter than the originals.
b.	they both are in modern style.
c.	each mocks and makes fun of its original.
d.	each is serious about its original.

Parody

Definition

The imitations of *The Rubaiyat of Omar Khayyam* and Thurber's "The Little Girl and the Wolf" are called parodies.

A parody is:

- a spoof on or imitation of another work.

- the imitation of the style of another work, writer or genre.

- dependant on exaggeration, on purpose.

- is for a comic or funny effect. The exaggeration usually creates the effect.

Exaggeration in Swift

You are going to look for exaggerations in Swift's poem.

➢ Use the table to help you sort out exaggerations.

➢ Read **Tips** below before you begin filling in the table.

Tips

As you again read Swift's poem, you will have flip back to the original Greek folktale. You are comparing the two.

In filling out the table on the next two pages, try to find the most comical or funniest things in the poem to use in the table.

- The **Exaggeration Category** are the important points to look for in the poem, for example, changes Swift made to the original characters of the Greek story. We have already listed a couple of them.

- In **Examples from the Poem**, fill in examples from the poem . Each example has to fit in the exaggeration category where you put it. The largest category is the transformations that occur to the house, the furniture, and the old couple. You should be able to find several funny examples of these.

There are two boxes at the end of the table for any categories with their examples that you can add.

Sort for exaggeration in Swift's poem

Exaggeration Category	Examples from the Poem
People	Greek gods become hermits/ Christian saints.
	Baucis is a yeoman.
Comical/Funny Words (Look for words in the poem *bolded and italicized* like this.)	"Farce" is the way the changes to the old folks can be described.
	Neighbors are called "churlish boors."
House and Setting	Poem is located in England.
	The old folks live in a cottage.
Transformations of the people and setting caused by the hermits	

Continued on next page

Sort for exaggeration in Swift's poem, Continued

Exaggeration Category	Examples from the Poem
Transformations in people and setting caused by the hermits, (continued)	
	Baucis and Philemon are comical as they become trees.
(Add your own category here.)	
(Add your own category here.)	

Summarize Swift's parody

Writing

Write about the way Swift parodied the original Greek folktale. Focus on the following:

> ➢ the changes Swift wrote into his poem

> and

> ➢ the transformations that the two saints caused in the actual story.

Read **Tips** below before you begin.

Tips

> ➢ Use the categories as part of your topic sentences.

> ➢ Use the examples from the poem to support or give details about your topic sentences.

You should have at least four paragraphs about what Swift did to create his parody.

God and a Little Bird

"Gjetrudsfuglen"
(from Norway)

In those days when our Lord and St. Peter went wandering about here on earth, they came once to a woman who sat and baked. She was called Gjertrud and had a red cap on her head. Since they had walked long and were both hungry the Lord asked Gjertrud very kindly for a taste of her pancake.

"Yes," said the old woman, "they could certainly have a bit." But when she took a little piece of dough and rolled it out, it grew so large that it filled the whole griddle. The pancake was too big.

"Well," thought Gjertrud, "He can't have this one." So she took an even smaller piece of dough, but as soon as she rolled it out and spread it on the griddle, this pancake was also too big.

"No," she thought, "he can't have this one either." This time, she took only a wee bit of dough, but the pancake was again much too big.

"Well, I really don't have anything to give you," said Gjertrud. "You'll just have to go your way, without even a little taste. All these pancakes are much too big!"

Continued on next page

God and a Little Bird, Continued

Then The Lord was angry and said: "Because you have treated me so poorly, you will have this punishment: You will be a bird and scratch for dry food between the bark and wood of the trees. You will only get a drop to drink whenever it rains!"

Scarcely had the Lord uttered the last word when the old woman became a woodpecker and, taking off from the breadboard, she flew up the chimney. And you can see her today flying around with her red cap, her body all black from the chimney soot. She hacks and pecks constantly at trees, looking for food and cheeps at rain clouds because she is always thirsty and is waiting for water. (We call this bird *woodpecker.)*

From: P. Chr. Asbjørnsen and J. Moe. *Norske Folke- og Huldre Eventyr i utvalg etter originaltekster 1852 og 1870*, selected by Trygve Knudsen. Oslo: Universitetsforlaget, 1964. pp. 10-11. (Translated by David Garnett)

Great Spirit and the Little Bird

A Native American Folktale

… Long ago the Great Spirit came down from the sky and talked with men. Once as he went up and down the earth, he came to the wigwam of a woman. He went into the wigwam and sat down by the fire, but he looked like an old man. … The woman did not know who he was.

"I have fasted for many days," said the Great Spirit to the woman. "Will you give me some food?" The woman made a very little cake and put it on the fire. "You can have this cake," she said, "if you will wait for it to bake."

"I will wait," said the Great Spirit.

When the cake was baked, the woman stood and looked at it. She thought, "It is very large. I thought it was small. I will not give him so large a cake as this." So she put it away and made a smaller one. "If you will wait, I will give you this one when it is baked," she said, and the Great Spirit said, "I will wait."

When the second cake was baked, it was larger than the first one. "It is so large that I will keep it for a feast," thought the old woman. So she said to her guest, "I will not give you this cake, but if you will wait, I will make you another one."

"I will wait," replied the Great Spirit again.

Then the woman made another cake from an even tinier piece. When she went to the fire for this third one, she found it the largest of all. She did not know that the Great Spirit's magic had made each cake larger and she thought, "This is a marvel, but I will not give away the largest cake of all." So she said to her guest, "I have no food for you. Go to the forest and look there for your food. You can find it in the bark of the trees, if you will."

Continued on next page

166

Great Spirit and the Little Bird, Continued

The Great Spirit was angry when he heard the words of the woman. He rose up from where he sat and threw back his cloak. "A woman must be kind and gentle," he said, "and you are selfish. You shall no longer be a woman and live in a wigwam. You shall go out into the forest and hunt for your food in the bark of trees."

The Great Spirit stamped his foot on the earth, and the woman grew smaller and smaller. Wings sprouted from her body, and feathers grew all over her. With a loud cry, she rose from the earth and flew away to the forest.

And to this day all woodpeckers live in the forest and hunt for their food in the bark of trees.

Adapted from: Florence Holbrook. *The Book of Nature Myths*. Boston: Houghton, Mifflin, and Company, 1902. Not in copyright. At: www.archive.org/details/bookofnaturemyth00holb

The Woman and the Little Bird

A Folktale from Finland

A beggar came to a house in the village of Ilmola and asked the woman there: "Make me a little bread."

The woman rolled a little ball of dough and put it in the oven to bake. The bread rose and puffed up and became big. The woman took out the bread, but didn't give it to the beggar. The beggar became sad, saying, "You didn't give me even a piece as you promised."

The woman replied, "I will make you another one a bit smaller." She made a second dough ball and put it on the highest shelf in the oven to bake, but it too swelled and got large. So the woman put this one aside on her bread board. Then the beggar said: "A sad outcome, you promised that one to me."

Then the woman said, "I will try to make another for you. Whatever happens, this one is yours." So she made a third one, very small, and put it in the oven. But this loaf turned into a swallow. It circled around the room. Just as it was taking off up the chimney, the old woman grabbed her bread knife and split the bird's tail feathers.

When the swallow reach the roof, he sang out: "The woman of Ilmola split my tale, God, knows this." From then on, swallows have split tail feathers.

Adapted from: Oskar Dähnhardt. *Natursagen. Eine Samlung naturdeutender Sagen, Märchen, Fabeln und Legenden,* 4 Bände. Berlin, 1907. At: www.archive.org/details/natursageneinesa04dhuoft (Translated by David Garnett)

Compare and contrast the three little bird folktales

What do you think

Do you see some immediate similarities and differences between these three folktales? Which of them seem more closely related?

To compare and contrast the three tales

> ➢ First read **Compare and Contrast: Remember!** below.
> ➢ Then fill in the **Compare and Contrast** organizer that follows after the next section.

Compare and Contrast: Remember!

Tips on Contrast

You are going to compare and contrast the three little bird folktales: "Gjertrudfuglen," the Native American folktale, and the folktale from Finland.

Importance of Trait or Action

In the case of the transformations, you have to compare and contrast or show a similarity and a difference on a general trait or action, such as the person who performed the transformation or the object of the transformation.

Common: Very Important in Contrast

A similarity or a difference has to come from something that is **common to the items you are contrasting**. If the comparison or the contrast is not based on a common trait or action in all three folktales, it is not a valid comparison or contrast and will make no sense.

As you can see, you have to figure out the general traits and actions that are common to the three little bird folktales. A trait or action:

- Is the baseline for your comparison or contrast.
- Guides you in what to look for, to compare or contrast in the three bird folktales.
- Is a general feature of all three folktales.
- Helps you sort the details of the items so that you can find the similarities and the differences. It is a way of organizing the similarities and the differences.

Do the exercise on the next page to help you understand trait and action when contrasting.

Continued on next page

Compare and Contrast: Remember!, Continued

Think of a jet and a twin-engine bi-plane. List all the different traits you can compare and contrast these two items on, to show how similar and different they are. We have started you with a couple. See if you can complete the table below.

(Write the traits below.)

Similarities for Comparison

i.	Both planes fly up and down in the air.
ii.	Both have wheels to land on.
iii.	
iv.	
v.	

Differences for Contrast

i	Size is a difference between a jet and a bi-plane.
ii.	
iii.	
iv.	
v.	

What to do

➤ Fill out the **Compare** section first, on the next page. Write a sentence by each number in the table that shows how the three tales are similar. This should not be difficult.

➤ Then fill out the **Contrast** part of the table.

Continue on next page

Compare and Contrast for the three little bird folktales

Compare
Write a sentence by each number about how **all**
three little bird folktales are alike or similar.

1.	
2.	
3.	
4.	
5.	
6.	
7.	
8.	
9.	
10.	
11.	
12.	

Continue on next page

Compare and Contrast for the three little bird folktales,
Continued

Contrast

Trait or Attribute of difference	Gjertruds-fuglen	Native Amer. Tale	Finnish Tale
1. A god or deity performs the transformation.	X	X	
2. Bread turns into a bird.			X
3.			
4.			
5.			
6.			
7.			
8.			
9.			
10.			

Decision   Based on your comparison and contrast, decide which of the two tales are more closely related. Which two show the greatest similarities?

_____

Write about your comparison and contrast

What to do

Write about your decision: Which of the two tales are probably more closely related? Which tale differs more from the other two?

Using the tables you have just filled in and the three folktales,

➢ First discuss the similarities among the three little bird folktales. This should be easy.

➢ Start the next paragraph by stating your decision about which two are more similar. Then use the work from the Contrast table to support your decision.

➢ Tell how two of them are different from the third.

Another Look

You could look at the little bird folktales from a different viewpoint or perspective. They are also "origin" folktales.

• "Gjertrudsfuglen" shows the origin of the woodpecker or **how** woodpeckers came to be.

• The Finnish folktale about the swallow tells about the origin of swallows' split tail feathers or **why** swallows have split tail feathers.

• What about the folktale of Babkis and Filomon from Turkey? Is it an origin folktale?

These "how" and "why" folktales are classified into categories by folklore researchers.

• Each type of tale in a specific category is given a number.
• Then if folklorists discover other folktales with these same traits, they put such new tales in the proper numbered category.

Chapter VII
Origins - How/Why Folktales

Introduction and Overview

Introduction	Do you remember the folktale "Gjertrudsfuglen?" It was a transformation tale: The Lord transformed Gjertrud into a woodpecker.
	The tale also explains how woodpeckers came into the world. In this chapter, you are going to explore more of these how/why origin stories.

What to do: **Lesson** **Objectives**	You will:

> Read various how/why folktales.

> Define and use implicit judgment in a character study.

> Complete a character study of one of the people in a folktale.

> Develop your own character, with explicit and implicit traits.

> Classify folktales as transformation or how/why origin tales.

Companion **Guide**	This workbook is a companion to *"Snipp snapp snute, så er eventyret ute" – Folklore Reader and Critical Thinking Workbook*, which has additional critical thinking materials and reading selections.

Continued on next page

Introduction and Overview, Continued

Lesson Content   The selections that you will read and write about in this chapter are:

- "The Devil as Deacon" from Bulgaria.

- "Legend of the Geranium" by Ada M. and Eleanor L. Skinner.

- "Lily of the Valley" by W. V. Burgess.

- "How Roses came first into the World" by Sir John Mandeville.

- Origin of the Forget-me-not from Germany.

- "Our Lady of the Little Glass" translated by Margaret Hunt.

Let's get started   You might think that the devil couldn't originate anything, but there are a number "r"eligious folktales in which he participates in the *how* or *why* of the story. Read one on the next page.

A Devilish How/Why - Origin Folktale

The Devil as Deacon
(from Bulgaria)

Once there was a bishop, whose first deacon was the devil himself. The bishop, however, never suspected this. He told the deacon everything and trusted him completely. This devil-deacon wrote in the religious book that the bishops were allowed to get married. When all the congregation learned about this, each brought a wedding gift to the bishop: one brought a ram; another, a [lamb]; still another, a chicken for roasting.

Now there was a poor old man. He took his scrawny, little cock [rooster], for he had nothing better to offer. He set off to take this a wedding gift to the bishop. Night came, and the old man decided to spend the night by a pear tree. He put the scrawny cock to sleep in the tree and lay down under the tree. About midnight, [some demons] came and climbed the pear tree. Suddenly one of the demons noticed the man lying under the tree, [They all began to talk] among themselves about whether to ask the man who he was.

The old man heard them and became very scared. So afraid was the old man that he gritted his teeth and pretended to be dead. The demons kicked him and rolled him around, but the old fellow didn't move. So the demons thought the old man was really dead and let him be.

Now when all the demons climbed the tree, the chief among them, the devil himself told them how he had written in the holy books that bishops were allowed to get married. All the other demons laughed and shrieked with glee and wished that they had done that. Suddenly, the scrawny rooster up and crowed. All the devils clambered down [climbed down] the pear tree and ran off, for when a cock crows – demons have to move out.

The old man, who had lain under the pear tree, had overheard the devil's speech. He got up, took his rooster and went on to see the bishop. When he came to the bishop's residence, he asked the deacon to go in and give the bishop his little rooster. The deacon told him the scrawny, little rooster was not a worthy gift for the bishop and that he wouldn't be allowed in. But finally, the bishop ordered that the old man be allowed to come in.

Continued on next page

A Devilish How/Why - Origin Folktale, Continued

 The old man entered and bowed respectfully to the bishop. ... Then the old man said, "Your highly respected bishop, I only want to hear from you if it is true that you want to get married."

"Yes, it is true," answered the bishop.

"How is this, your eminence?" continued the old man. "I have heard that a bishop who married cannot stay in God's service. So how does it stand now? This can't be such a simple matter."

"Easy," answered the bishop. "If it is written in the holy books that bishops are not allowed to marry, then I will not get married. If it is not a sin, I can get married."

"So you don't know that the devil has written this and that the devil himself is your chief deacon!" answered the old man.

How can that be?" replied the bishop. "He is my most trusted confidante and has helped me at all the holy services in church."

"I know he is the devil," continued the old man. Just last night, I heard with my own ears how he himself told the other demons that he had written it in the holy books to cause you a lot of trouble." Then the old man told the bishop the whole story.

"How can this be?" said the bishop. "The deacon has always assisted me at all services."

"Has he been present during the whole service? At the communion, for example?"

"I haven't taken that much notice," replied the bishop.

"Well, your eminence, tomorrow conduct a service, but be sure to lock all the doors, close all the windows, and shut all the cupboards so that there is no way out of the church. When you perform communion, pay attention to what happens to the deacon."

Think about: Why might the old man ask the priest to close everything up during the service?

Continued on next page

A Devilish How/Why - Origin Folktale, Continued

The bishop did as the old man said. He performed the holy liturgy the next morning. When he came to the communion prayer, the devil ran to the door and tried to open it. When he couldn't, he rushed around to the windows, pulling and pushing on them to open them, but he couldn't get out. He was in a panic!

As the communion prayer continued, the devil began to burst open and a whole crowd of mice jumped out of the devil. And that's how mice came into the world!

And the bishop? Well, he understood how it was and remained unmarried.

> Adapted from: August Leskien. *Balkanmärchen aus Bulgarien*, Jena, Austria, 1919. Not in copyright. at: http://www.sagen.at/index.html (Translated by David Garnett)

An Interesting Character?

The old man in this folktale is a very interesting character. As opposed to the devil, whose mischievous character is very clear and straightforward from the beginning of the folktale, the old man may be more than just an old man with a scrawny rooster.

You are going to do a short character study of the old man with the scrawny rooster. Before you begin, read about how to do a character study below.

Character Study: Two Parts

What to do

In this section, you will look at the old man with the scrawny rooster. Try to figure out what kind of person the old man is from his behavior in the folktale.

You do more than just look at the character in relation to the plot; you look at all aspects of the character: both

- what is obvious

  and

- what is not so obvious.

This project will take a bit of concentration.

- You need to take your time to complete it.
- You should do the work a little at a time.

Continued on next page

Character Study: Two Parts, Continued

**Part I :
Character
Study from the
Folktale**

This section has two parts. In the first, you are going to:

➢ Do a character study of the old man with the scrawny rooster.

➢ Analyze the character by using a **Matrix for Implied Judgment** thinking organizer.

➢ Write a character study of the old man, based on your completed **Matrix for Implied Judgment** thinking organizer and the folk tale.

**Part II: Create
your own
character**

In the second part of this character study section, you will:

➢ Develop your own character using **Character Development for your own Character**.

➢ Write a biography of your new character, using your completed thinking organizer.

Implicit and Explicit in a Character

Two Key Points

An author tells about a character in two main ways: explicit traits and implicit or implied traits.

**Explicit
Statements**

In the case of explicit traits or attributes or explicit characteristics, the author gives direct information and interpretive comments about the character. The narrator might:

- Describe the character's clothing, hair, eyes, etc.
- Tell about actions that the character does.
- Have the character directly say something that tells about her/himself.
- Give the thoughts that the character has.
- State what the character likes and dislikes, or how the character feels about another person or thing in the story.

The author directly explains these things. The reader doesn't really have to do anything except read.

Continued on next page

Implicit and Explicit in a Character, Continued

Implicit Statements and Implied Judgment

Here the author doesn't directly state something about the character.

- The author tells you, the reader, in a description, example, thought, etc., about the character.
- You make a judgment about the character based on the description, action, etc.

This is called implied judgment and allows a narrator to:

- Tell about an attitude or thought of a character without directly labeling it.
- Give an impression of the character and asks the reader to interpret the character from the impression.

Example

Instead of saying a person is a glutton, the author describes how the boy gobbles up globs of food, using his hands and slobbering all over his mouth and chin. The author never says that the character is a glutton.

The author implies (never directly states) that the character is a glutton from the "piggy-like" description. You, the reader, come to the conclusion about the character's gluttony, by figuring out what the author means from his description. You get at the character from what the author implies, not directly states, about the character:

> **Again, this is called implied judgment. You, the reader, make a judgment about the character based on the author's implication or implicit statement. Nothing directly is said about the character of the person, in this case the boy, but the description implies that he is a glutton.**

You will use implied judgment a lot in reading fiction.

Another Example

J. R. R. Tolkien's descriptions of Golum in the Ring trilogy show how he implies about this character.

- Tolkien never directly states that Golum is evil.
- He just let's Golum talk about himself and life and describes Golum's actions and feelings in relation to the ring.

Using implied judgment, you get the idea from all that Tolkien writes about Golum that the creature really is evil – and pitiful.

Use implied judgment with the old man

Use a matrix   You will use the matrix that follows to figure out some of the
possible, implied things about the old man with the scrawny
chicken. First, read **Tips** below.

Tips
- ➤ Put what the old man says, does, or how he is described in
  under **What the old man says or does or how he is
  described**.

- ➤ Then under **What might be implied**, write what you think the
  statement you have written in the first column implies about
  the character of the old man.

- ➤ You will need to think carefully about everything that the old
  man was involved in, how he behaved, what he said, etc., to
  see if there is something implied about him.

We have started the matrix. You try to finish it.

Matrix for Implied Judgment for the Old Man

What the old man says or does or how he is described	What might be implied
The old man is thin.	He fasts and doesn't eat much. Perhaps he is religious.
The old man "gritted his teeth and pretended to be dead."	
The old man says, **"Has he [the devil] been present during the whole service? At the communion …?"**	The old man knows about religion and can talk about the religious service with a bishop of the church.
The old man says, **"… Close all the windows … shut all the cupboards so that there is no way out of the church."** He gives the bishop a lot of advice.	

Writing   Using your completed matrix and the folktale, write a short character study of the old man. Be sure to include:

 ➢ Explicit points about the old man.
 ➢ Implicit ideas about him that you thought of from the tale.
 ➢ In the last paragraph, write about who you think the old man might really be.

Support all you ideas with examples from the folktale.

Develop your own character

You have looked at the character of the old man. Now you are going to develop your own character. To do this, you will use a **Character Development** organizer on the next page. First read **Tips** below.

Requirements There are a number of points that you need to include in your character, to make him/her complete.

The character which you created can be a person, an animal, a fantastic being, etc. Your character must :

- Move on its own
- Speak
- Act and do things
- Have a definite physical description with traits and characteristics.

Read **Tips** below.

Tips You must include:

➢ definite explicit characteristics, such as size, color, etc.,

and

➢ implicit traits about which a reader needs to make implied judgment.

Take a look back at all the "r"eligious folklore folks and critters you have met. Some of them did and said some really interesting things. They may give you clues about your own character.

Now, using the table on the next page develop your character.

Character Development

ABILITIES/ACTIONS: What does the character do – important actions!

1.

2.

3.

4.

FEELS/EMOTIONS: How does this character feel - attitudes, feelings!

1.

2.

3.

4.

What is the name of your character?
_____

LOOKS/APPEARANCE: What are the important physical traits of your character?

1.

2.

3.

4.

SAYS/SPEECH: What your character says – important things!

1.

2.

3.

4.

Write up your character

A Final Review

Now that you have completed the **Character Development** organizer:

➢ Go back and check out **Tips** before the organizer to be sure you have included all the requirements for your character.

➢ Now read **About Organizing your writing** below before you begin writing out your character.

About organizing your writing

First Paragraph. Introduce your character with its name. You can also tell where the character comes from and anything about its family. The appearance of the character might fit in here too. This is general information.

Second Paragraph

➢ Here you might put something about the character's actions and abilities. You may want to describe each and give an example. If the character is brave, you could give an event where he/she showed bravery.

➢ If there was an exciting incident that your character was part of, here would be the place to write about this.

Third Paragraph. A little about the attitude and make up of the character. For example, is he kind or stingy? Does he make friends easily? Why or why not!

Fourth Paragraph. This is where you tell about what the character says, including his opinions about his life and world.

In **the last paragraph**, tell if you would like to have this character as your friend. Explain.

How/Why - Origin "r"eligious folktales: Flowers

Introduction

"If one finds oneself with bread in both hands, that person should exchange one loaf for some flowers of the narcissus, because the loaf feeds the body, but the flowers feed the soul."

Koran

"As from a large heap of flowers many garlands and wreaths are made; so by a mortal in this life, there is much good work to be done."

Buddha

"All men are like grass, and all their glory is like the flowers of the field; the grass withers and the flowers fall."

Holy Bible, Peter 1:24

There are probably thousands of quotes in all the religions of the world about flowers: For example, flowers have been used to teach humility, to explain love, to define purity. They are firmly woven into the doctrine of most religions.

Flowers have also played a part in the "r"eligious folklore that follows the major religions. You are going to read a number of how/why flower folktales.

Think about …

You have already read a number of origin folktales as well as some transformation tales. As you read the folktales that follow, try to decide what kind of tales they are: how/why tales, origin, or transformation folktales. Later you will classify these tales.

Let's start with a flower folktale about the Prophet Muhammad. It is a simple tale. What might you call the change in the folktale?

Holy Folk and Flowers

Legend of the Red Geranium
Ada M. Skinner and Eleanor L. Skinner

Once upon a time there lived in a country far over the sea a prophet whose name was Mohammed. He was a great leader and traveled many miles through his country, teaching the people who looked to him for guidance.

One scorching [sun-burning] hot day, after a long pilgrimage through a dusty country, the great prophet stopped to rest. A clear stream flowed near him, and Mohammed bathed in its cool waters and then washed his travel-stained clothes. He spread the clean linen over a tall mallow plant. Then he lay down to rest while his garments [clothes] were drying.

After sleeping for an hour or two the prophet wakened [woke up], much refreshed. He lifted his dry linen from the common plant, and lo! a great surprise met his eye. The mallow had been changed into a magnificent geranium, whose red clusters were dazzlingly bright in the sunshine.

> **Note**: A mallow is a small plant like a hibiscus. It is stubby and short and often grows in swamps.

From: Ada M. Skinner and Eleanor L. Skinner. T*he Turquoise Storybook: Stories and Legends of Summer and Nature*. New York: Duttfield and Company, 1919. Not in copyright. At: http://www.archive.org/stream/turquoisestorybo00skin/turquoisestorybo00skin_djvu.txt

Think about: What kind of tale is this? Transformation? How/why? Or maybe both?

A Saint and his Flowers

Now read another tale about an English saint and his relationship to flowers. Keep in mind the kind of tale you are reading.

"Lily of the Valley"
W. V. Burgess

Saint Leonard of Sussex, whose valiant fame
Is writ [written] down in annals [stories] of saintly lore,
[He was] ... one who to his fellows did restore
Safety and peace.

Continued on next page

Holy Folk and Flowers, Continued

A Saint and his Flowers

From the forest there came
At divers [various] times, a dragon with eyes aflame,
And gorey [bloody] maw [mouth], for victims, more and more.
Until the folk despairing did implore
The saint to oust [get rid of] the beast, in God's good name.

The holy man put on his sword and hood.
And after toilsome [hard working] fight, the monster slew.

And in the glades and fastnesses [firm places] ,we're told,
Wherever the saint was wounded and his blood
Sprinkled the ground, there lilies of the valley
Upgrew [grew up].

> From: W. V. Burgess. *One Hundred Sonnets, Prefaced by an Essay on the Sonnet's history and place in English verse.* Manchester: Sherratt and Hughes, 1901. Not in copyright. At: http://www.archive.org/stream/ onehundredsonnet00burgrich/onehundredsonnet00burgrich_ djvu.txt

---

Mini-exercise

Complete the study tables about this poem and the earlier folktale about Muhammad. Follow the directions in each table.

Looking at the folktale "Legend of the Geranium" and the poem "Lily of the Valley," you might say _____

(Circle **all the letters** that apply.)

a.	Lily of the Valley is an origin story.
b.	Lily of the Valley is not a transformation story as nothing is changed.
c.	"Legend of the Geranium" may not be an origin story.
d.	"Legend of the Geranium" is a transformation story.

Continued on next page

Holy Folk and Flowers, Continued

As opposed to the transformation of Baucis and Philemon, where Zeus changed the old couple to trees, in "Lily of the Valley,"

_____
(Circle **the letter** that applies.)

a.	an angel made the transformation of St. Leonard's blood.
b.	it is a wonderful mystery how his blood changed to flowers.
c.	St. Leonard himself made the change.
d.	the dragon effected the change to flowers.

Sir John Mandeville's folktale

This next folktale is from an English knight, who traveled to Istanbul and the Holy Land in the 14th century. He kept a kind of journal of his travels and the various events he witnessed and heard about.

"Chapter IX: How roses came first into the world"
Sir John Mandeville

[Here, near the monastery of St. Catherine in the Sinai] ... is the field Floridus, that is to say, the 'field flourished.' .... Supposedly, a ... young girl was ... wrongly accused and ... was condemned to death, to be burned in that field. [So she] ... was led out and [tied to a stake on a pile of wood]. As the fire began to burn about her, she ... [prayed] to the Lord, saying, "Lord, I am not guilty of the sin they accuse me of. Help me."

When she had thus spoken, the torch was put to the wood, and the fire rose about the girl. Then suddenly, the fire was quenched [extinguished] and [went] out. The brands [pieces of wood] that were burning became red rose trees, and the brands that were not [yet on fire] became white rose trees – all of them full of roses. These then were the first rose trees with roses, both white and red ... . This maiden was saved ... . That field was full of roses.

From: *The Travels of Sir John Mandeville*. At:
http://www.romanization.com/books/mandeville/chap09.html

Continued on next page

Holy Folk and Flowers, Continued

Jesus and a Flower

This is one of the many folktales about how the flower, forget-me-not, came to be. In one version of the folktale, as Eve was leaving the Garden of Eden, she began to say Good-bye to all the flowers and plants there. As she went out the gate to join Adam, a little voice was supposed to have piped up, saying, "For get me not." So that is supposed to be one "origin" of the flower. Below you will read another version.

Origin of Forget-me-not
(from Germany)

When Jesus was a child, he would often sit in his mother's lap. One day, he was sitting and looking up at his mother's blue eyes. "How I wish," he thought to himself, "that all little children could see my mother's eyes. How beautiful they are. I don't want to forget them."

Jesus reached up and touched Mary's eyes. Then he waved his hand over the ground. Suddenly, where nothing but bare earth had been, blue forget-me-nots sprang up. That is the origin of the flower called forget-me-not.

Adapted from: http://en.wikipedia.org/wiki/Forget-me-not#The_name (Not in copyright.)

A German Tale

The "r"eligious folktale that follows is from a folktale collection by the Brothers, Wilhelm and Jacob Grimm. Both brothers were university professors, who spent many years collecting folktales from everyday people of Germany in the 19th century. Their work became the model for many later folklore collectors.

Continued on next page

Holy Folk and Flowers, Continued

Mary and a Flower

"Our Lady's Little Glass"
translated by Margaret Hunt

[369] Once upon a time a waggoner's [wagon driver's] cart which was heavily laden [loaded] with wine had stuck so fast that in spite of all that he could do, he could not get it to move again. Then it chanced [happened] that Our Lady [Mary] just happened to come by that way. … When she … [saw] the poor man's distress, she said to him, "I am tired and thirsty, give me a glass of wine, and I will set … [your] cart free for … [you]."

"Willingly," answered the waggoner, "but I have no glass in which I can give you the wine."

Then Our Lady plucked a little white flower with red stripes, called field bindweed, which looks very [much] like a glass, and gave it to the wagoner. He filled it with wine, and then Our Lady drank it. .. In the self-same instant, the cart was set free, and the waggoner could drive onward. The little flower is still always called *Our Lady's Little Glass*.

From: Margaret Hunt. *Grimm's Household Tales*, 1884. Not in copyright. At: http://www.mainlesson.com/display.php?author=hunt&book=grimm&story=ladyglass&PHPSESSID=5659b542180dc1f924360a00dc467b23

Transformation? or How/Why - Origin?

Your Turn

You are going to classify a number of folktales. Before you start, let's look at two more "r"eligious folktales to be sure you understand the basic difference between origin and transformation. You need to decide if each is a transformation tale or an origin tale.

Continued on next page

Transformation? or How/Why - Origin?, Continued

Which is it?

When Jesus was about five years old, he found not a crumb of bread in the house. So he began to cry. Mary said to him: "Child, go into the village and beg; perhaps folks there will give you something to stifle [stop] your hunger."

So the young Jesus went into the village and knocked on many doors. But no one had any food left over; everyone had so little. Finally, he came to a little bakery. Besides the baker himself, Jesus found two women there. One of them shouted: "Look here at this cute little boy. What is your name, sweet little thing?"

"My name is Jesus."

"What a name, and where's your home?" she continued.

"My mother is Mary."

"And what is your father's name?"

"Joseph, the carpenter," answered Jesus.

"And where is your family from?"

"My mother is from Nazareth."

So, child, what do you want here?" she asked again.

"I am so hungry, and my mother didn't have any bread. Please, give me a little bit," replied Jesus.

The dough for the two women lay right there on the bread board. The baker was about to cut it. Then one of the women told the baker, "Wait a moment, I would like you to bake a flat cake for this kid."

Then the other woman interrupted, " Doesn't it seem right to you that we both give a piece of our dough so that the flat bread is bigger? My piece would just keep him full."

The first woman, however, was a bit stingy and said: " So, if you want a bigger piece for the kid, I might as well bake mine separate."

The generous woman cut a fine piece of dough, filled it with cheese bits and little sweet beans and said to Jesus: "Go and [play a while]. It will be ready soon."

Continued on next page

Transformation? or How/Why - Origin?, Continued

The stingy woman cut off a little piece, filled it with garlic. Then the baker baked both loaves. When both breads came out of the oven, the kind women shouted, "Look how beautiful my bread has risen," and said to Jesus: "Here child, take it all and go quickly to your mother. Both of you have flat bread to eat now!" Then she kissed Jesus.

The stingy woman was annoyed that she also had a large bread and said, "Equal for equal—a little boy should only get a little bread." And she cut a meager bit from her flat bread with a sharp knife and gave it to little Jesus.

Jesus rushed home and gave his mother the breads. When she asked him how to reward the two women for their gifts, he said, "The kind woman gave me a real gift, she gave me the best she had: Cheese and sweet beans. For this, her children will be with me in heaven when they die, and every day she will eat better than cheese and beans."

"The stingy woman gave with an unwilling heart. It was a mean gift. It would have been better for her to show me the door than to give me that little crust. For this, she will carry the smell of her garlic about, all her days and pass it on to her children. People will avoid them all. And when they die, only garlic will grow by their graves. They will never be quit of the stink."

Since that time, garlic smells good as long as it is raw, but it spoils people's breath. And whoever smells from the mouth and nose is one of the offspring of that stingy woman.

Adapted from: Oskar Dahnhardt. *Natur Sagen: Eine Sammlung Naturdeütender Sagen Märchen Fabeln Und Legenden*. Berlin, 1909. Not in copyright. At http://www.archive.org/stream/natursageneinesa02duoft/natursagenein esa02duoft_djvu.txt (translated by David Garnett)

Think about: Which kind of "r"eligious folktale is this. How/why origin or transformation? Explain why you think this.

Now read the next folktale from Poland about a famous queen. Which kind of folktale is it?

Continued on next page

Transformation? or How/Why - Origin?, Continued

Which is it?

The Legend of Jadwiga

Jadwiga, who as queen of Poland, was a devout Christian. [She] often smuggled food from the castle, to the poor, out the back door of the castle. [She carried the foods] in her large apron.

Jadwiga's husband, Jagiello, who as king of Poland, was a very suspicious man. ... Jagiello's men, playing on his mistrusting mind, told him of his bride's strange comings and goings, thus throwing doubt upon her intentions. His advisors had him thinking she was taking secrets to rebels. Jagiello was determined to get to the bottom of this accusation.

One night, as [the queen] was leaving by a secret door, Jagiello sprang out of the bushes and demanded to see what was in Jadwiga's apron. When Jadwiga opened her apron, a garland of roses lay there, not a morsel of food. To this day, Jadwiga is always depicted wearing an apron of roses.

Adapted from: http://www.angelfire.com/mi4/polcrt/LegendJadwiga.html

---

Writing

Decide what kind of folk tale the two "r"eligious folktales you have just read is, how/why origin or transformation.

Write about you decision:

➢ Tell which tale is an origin tale. Explain why.

➢ Then tell which tale is a transformation tale. Explain your reasons.

Classifying again

With the difference between a transformation tale and a how/why origin tale in mind, let's go back and do a bit of classification of folktales. Start with **Classification** on the next page.

Classification

Do you remember the classification you did in **Chapter I** about the different places of worship? You classified the different activities and actions that went on in a place of worship. There was also the section about classifying triangles.

> ➤ You are going to do a similar classification of many of the folktales you have read up to this point. You will use the **Sort** classification organizer on the next page to sort out the folktales.

> ➤ Read about the organizer and how to fill it out, in **Tips** below.

Tips The folktales you will use in your classification work are listed in **Sort** on the next page.

You should go back and skim these folktales so that you can remember them in relation to origin and transformation. Then fill out the table this way:

Beside the description or title of the tale **check**:

> ➤ Under **How/Why Origin Tale?** if the tale is a how or why tale, about how something started or originated. It might help to write down what was created originated by the check in the table – this way you can easily remember what it was.

> ➤ Under **Transformation(s) in tale?** if the tale has any transformations in it. You may want to jot down what the transformation was in the table as we did.

> ➤ Under **Neither?** if the tale has **no** origins and **no** transformation in it.

<u>Note</u>:

- Some tales may be only how/why origin tales; others may be only transformation tales.
- A number may be both how/why origin tales and transformation folktales.
- A few might have no origin and no transformations in them.

We have filled in some of the table; you finish it.

Sort for Origin and Transformation

Chapt. Number	Tale	How/Why Origin Tale?	Transforma-tion(s) in tale?	Neither?
II	**Solomon and Asmodeus**			X
II	**"The Gnome who built a church"** (See last paragraph of tale.)			
II	**"The Devil's Church Building"** (See last paragraph of tale.)			
III	**"The Quest for Sangraal"** by Hawker (See last section)			
IV	**St. Perpetua's Dream** (See the old white haired man.)		X (milk to cheese)	
V	**St. David and the Dragon**		X (milk to cheese)	
VI	**"Baucis and Philemon"** by Bulfinch			
VI	**Turkish tale about olive tree**			
VI	**"Baucis and Philemon"** by J. Swift			
VI	**"Gjertrudsfuglen"** from Norway			
VI	**Great Spirit and the Little Bird** (a Native American folktale)			
VI	**The Woman and the Little Bird** from Finland			
VII	**"Devil as Deacon"**			
VII	**"Legend of the Red Geranium"**			
VII	**"Lily of the Valley"**			
VII	**"How Roses came into World"**			
VII	**Origin of the Forget-me-not**			
VII	**"Our Lady of the Little Glass"**			

Your Classification for the Folktales

Writing

With your completed sort, write about your classification of the folktales. Read **Organize your writing** below to help you get started.

Organize your writing

➢ Start by introducing the folktales in a general way. Write about the topic of this writing: classification of folktales, including the two main categories of your classification.

➢ Discuss the tales that only have transformations in the next paragraph.

➢ Then follow up with a discussion of only the origin tales.

➢ Those tales that are both transformation and origin should be in the fourth paragraph.

➢ In the fifth paragraph, discuss the tales which are neither origin nor transformation.

➢ A final paragraph should give some conclusion about which group is the largest group with the most folktales and which group is the smallest with the least number of folktales.

Your Turn: Write your own how/why - origin story

What to do

Now write your own how to/why origin story.

➢ You can choose anything to originate in your story.
➢ The only requirement is that the story makes sense.

Chapter VIII
Active and Ascetic

Introduction and Overview

Definition

Two new words for you: *Active* and *Ascetic*.

We are not going to define them for you. Instead, you are going to read about two religious women from the *Holy Bible*. From their characters and attitudes, you should get a definition of these two new words.

**What to do:
Learning
Objectives**

➢ Contrast the characters of Mary and Martha.

➢ Write your one definition of an *ascetic*, based on your analysis of Mary and Martha.

➢ Write your one definition of an *active person*, based on your analysis of Mary and Martha.

➢ Based on your definition of *ascetic* and *active*, classify characters in various other "r"eligious folktales of this volume as either *ascetic* or *active*.

**Companion
Guide**

This volume is a companion to *"Snipp snapp snute, så er eventyret ute" – Folklore Reader and Critical Thinking Workbook*, which has additional critical thinking materials and reading selections.

Continued on next page

Introduction and Overview, Continued

Chapter Components

A text or group of selections that you will read. Most of the writing and other work you do require you to read and refer to these text resource(s).

Any of a number of activities or exercises which you need to complete. These activities may include:

- Vocabulary exercises.
- Questions to answer.
- Study tables to complete
- Thinking organizers (graphic or picture diagrams) to fill out.
- Written work to plan, organize, and write.

All these activities should help you to read and understand the texts or to write about them. You may have to complete a project, which requires limited research.

Content

The selections you are going to read include:

- Luke 10:38-42 from the *Holy Bible*.

- "The Gospel Women -- Mary" by George MacDonald.

- "The Gospel Women -- Martha" by George MacDonald.

Mary and Martha: A Striking Contrast

A Brave Woman

Do you remember St. Martha, who subdued the dragoness Tarasque? That little folktale shows something very important about Martha's character and outlook on life. Read, again, the selection from the *Holy Bible* about Martha. As you read

> ➤ Pay attention to how both Martha and her sister, Mary, behave.
> ➤ Consider also what Jesus says to Martha about Mary. This is important too.

Luke 10:38-42
(New International Version)

38As Jesus and his disciples were on their way, he came to a village where a woman named Martha opened her home to him. 39She had a sister called Mary, who sat at the Lord's feet listening to what he said. 40But Martha was distracted [busy with] by all the preparations that had to be made. She came to him and asked, "Lord, don't you care that my sister has left me to do the work by myself? Tell her to help me!"

41"Martha, Martha," the Lord answered, "you are worried and upset about many things, 42but only one thing is needed. Mary has chosen what is better, and it will not be taken away from her."

Think about: What is **the** difference between Martha and Mary that Jesus emphasized?

Two Poems about Mary and Martha

- You are going to read two poems about these two Biblical women. The two poems about Martha and Mary were written by a 19th century English writer named George MacDonald. He is famous for a number of fantasies and fairy tales that he wrote, especially for young people.

- As you read these two poems, see how MacDonald expands on and embroiders on the character and attitudes of these two sisters.

Continued on next page

Mary and Martha: A Striking Contrast, Continued

"The Gospel Women -- Mary"
George MacDonald

1.

She sits at the Master's [Jesus'] feet
In motionless employ [not doing anything];   *Mary is doing something, what is it?*
Her ears, her heart, her soul complete
Drinks in the tide of joy.

She is the earth, and Jesus, the sun;
He shines forth on her leaves;   *What has Mary found from Jesus?*
She, in new life from darkness won,
Gives back what she receives. ...

The life from Jesus' voice she drinks like wine;
His word in her an echo found;
Her ear hears the world, where thought divine   *What does Jesus do with divine thought?*
was created ... in sound.

Her holy eyes, brimful of light,
Shine all unseen and low;
As if His radiant words all night   *How are Jesus' words described?*
Forth at those orbs [eyes] would go.

[At] the open door is Martha's face
Of anxious household state:
"Don't you care, Jesus," ... [Martha] says, "for my case,
That I alone should [on you] wait?"

Mary lifts her eyes
To Him, who calmly heard;
[She is ready now] ... to arise,
And go, before the word.

Mary's fear is banished [goes away] by his voice,
Her fluttering hope set free:
"This is", says Jesus, "Mary's choice,
She shall remain with me."

Oh, joy to every doubting heart,
Doing what she would,   *What is Mary's choice? What does Jesus say about it?*
If He, the Holy, take [her] part,
And call [her] ... choice the good!

Continued on next page

Mary and Martha: A Striking Contrast, Continued

2.

His [Jesus'] words are poured
Into her lonely ears;
But many guests are at the board,
And many tongues Mary hears.

With sacred foot [Mary] ... comes slow,
With daring, trembling tread;
With shadowing worship she bends low
Above the godlike head.

[Mary] ... breaks the box, the honoured thing!   *What is the final action Mary does?*
The ointment she pours a main [by hand];
Her priestly hands anoint her King,
And He shall live and reign. ...

From: George MacDonald. *A Hidden Life and Other Poems*. New York: Scribner,
           Armstrong, and Company,1872. Not in copyright. At:
           http://www.archive.org/details/hiddenlifeotherp00macd

---

Mini-exercise   Complete the study tables; follow the directions in each table.

Look at the following quotations from the poem (they are **bolded and italicize**
like this in the selection.)

"Her holy eyes, brimful of light, ..."

"With sacred foot [Mary] ... comes slow ..."

"Her priestly hands anoint her King, ..."

These three quotations compare Mary to a/an _____

(Circle **all the letters** that apply.)

a.	angel.
b.	priest.
c.	goddess.
d.	Jesus.

Continued on next page

201

Mary and Martha: A Striking Contrast, Continued

The primary image or picture of Jesus is the _____

(Circle **all the letters** that apply.)

a.	well from which Mary gets the water of her life.
b.	tree branch on which Mary, as an apple, grows.
c.	sun, which shines on Mary, who is the earth.
d.	mother bird feeding her little one, Mary.

A Poem about Martha   As you read this poem, also by George MacDonald, find the differences the poet describes between the two sisters.

"The Gospel Women – Martha"
George MacDonald

With joyful pride her heart is high:
Her humble house doth [does] hold
The man [Jesus] her nation's prophecy
Long ages hath [has] foretold!

What does Martha think of Jesus?

Poor, is he [Jesus]? Yes, and lowly born:
Her woman-soul is proud
To know and hail the coming morn
Before the eyeless crowd.

At her poor table will he [Jesus] eat?
He shall be served there
With honour and devotion meet
For any king that were!

How will Martha treat Jesus?

'Tis all she can; she does her part,
Profuse [abundant] in sacrifice;
Nor dreams that in her unknown heart
A better offering lies.

But many crosses she must bear;
Her plans are turned and bent [are not right];
Do what she can, things will not wear [go]
The form of her intent [the way she wants].

What kind of a time does she have serving?

Continued on next page

Mary and Martha: A Striking Contrast, Continued

With idle hands and drooping lid,
… Mary sits at rest!   *What does Martha think of her sister, Mary?*
Shameful her sister did
No service for their guest!

"Dear Martha, [says Jesus] one day Mary's lot [attitude]
Must rule thy hands and eyes;
You, Martha, all … your household cares forgot,
Must sit as idly wise! …

From: George MacDonald. *A Hidden Life and Other Poems*. New York: Scribner,
Armstrong, and Company,1872. Not in copyright. At:
http://www.archive.org/details/hiddenlifeotherp00macd

Jesus definitely feels one sister is better in outlook and attitude than the other. **Who is it?**
How do you know? Explain below. (Look as the *stanza* above for clues.)

Mini-exercise   Complete the study tables. Follow the directions in each table.

In contrast to Mary, Martha seems to be _____

(Circle **all the letters** that apply.)

a.	bustling about.
b.	not thinking too much.
c.	foolish.
d.	stressed out and complaining.

Continued on next page

Mary and Martha: A Striking Contrast, Continued

On the other hand, Mary seems to _____

(Circle **all the letters** that apply.)

a.	be very involved with religion.
b.	be thoughtful and silent.
c.	play dumb so she won't have to work.
d.	radiate [send out] a special kind of joy.

Remember the Divine Ladder of John Climacus in Chapter III. Who of the two sisters would probably climb the ladder first?

(Circle **all the letters** that apply.)

a.	Martha would probably climb it first because she is active.
b.	Mary would climb it because she can't keep still.
c.	Mary would climb it before Martha because Mary was listening.
d.	Mary would climb it first because she loved the Lord .

Martha and Mary: Define *ascetic* and *active*

What to do

Do you remember the words you first met at the beginning of this chapter -- *ascetic* and *active*?

You are going to develop your own definition of these two words by contrasting the:

- character and attitude of Martha with
- the character and attitude of Mary,

using the two poems of George MacDonald.

You will use a number of tables that follow to help you organize your thinking about the two sisters.

Continued on next page

Martha and Mary: Define *ascetic* and *active,* Continued

Words

- One of the ways to contrast the characters of Martha and Mary is by the descriptive words MacDonald uses for each sister.

- You may have already noticed a distinct difference in the vocabulary (words) he used to describe them. You will use this difference as a basis for writing about Martha and Mary.

The **Sort** matrix that follows should help you list the words.
In the **Sort** matrix:

- ➢ List all the words that are used to describe Mary in the first column.

- ➢ Then list all the words used to describe Martha.

- ➢ After each word, write which poem you got the word from.

- ➢ Just list the words in order from each poem.

Sort for Mary and Martha

Words about Mary	Which Poem?		Words about Martha	Which Poem?
Motionless	"Mary"		Anxious	"Mary"
Gives back	"Mary"		Waiting on someone	"Mary"
			Sacrifice	"Martha"
			Pride	"Martha"
			Proud	"Martha"
Idle	"Martha"			
Resting	"Martha"			

Guidance: Active and Ascetic Category Table

Another Table   Below is another table. This one helps you to group all the different descriptive words about the two sisters. It will help give you the main categories to write about when you start your definition of *ascetic* and *active*. Read **Active and Ascetic Category Table: Procedure** below, before you start to fill in the table.

Active and Ascetic Category Table: Procedure

Step	Action: What you do
1.	Put each word from **Sort for Mary and Martha** on the previous page into the table **Active and Ascetic Categories** on the next page. Each word on separate line of the table.
2.	Then decide if the word you have just listed fits better under **Active** or *Ascetic*.
3.	Check the box under the category where the word best fits. For: • **Active**, check either Action/Motion or Social/ Emotion, where the word seems best to belong. • *Ascetic*, check either *Thinking/Learning* or *Joy/Love*.
	<u>Note</u>: There is room in the table for you to put in your own categories under *Ascetic* and **Active**: two spaces for two *Ascetic* categories and two spaces for two **Active** categories. Fill them in if you feel a category which you got from the poems is missing.

Continued on next page

Active and Ascetic Category Table

Word (Person)	Active		Ascetic	
	Action/ Motion	Social/Emotion	*Thinking/Listening*	*Joy/Love*
Quiet (Mary)			*x*	
Shining (Mary)				*x*
Talking (Martha)		x		
Word/Person	Write beside **1.** And **2.** your own categories for **Active.**		Write beside *3.* And *4.* your own categories for *Ascetic.*	
	1.	**2.**	*3.*	*4.*

Write your own definition of *ascetic* and *active*

What to do

Using your completed **Active and Ascetic Categories** and the two poems by MacDonald, write up your own definition of *ascetic* and *active*. You will need to include the following in your writing:

➢ A statement in the first paragraph about the purpose for your writing, i.e., what you are writing about.

➢ A paragraph about an ascetic (person):
  • It must clearly show the important distinctions or traits of an ascetic.
  • You have to use examples from the poems to support your definition. Use the sister who is an ascetic as part of your examples.

➢ A paragraph about what an active person is:
  • Be sure to distinguish the active person from the ascetic.
  • Use examples in your definition. Be sure to include the sister who is the active person here.

➢ In the final paragraph, summarize with your own definition of *ascetic* and *active*.

Other Ascetics and Active Persons you have met

Now, let's go back to look at other people in "r"eligious folklore whom you have read about, up to this point. We have listed some of them in the table You need to review the tales up to this point:

1. Look at each character.

2. Determine if each is :

  • **Ascetic,**

  • *Active,*

    or

  • **Both.**

3. Check the appropriate box beside the character's name.

  <u>Note</u>: You may not be able to determine anything ascetic or active about some of the characters. Don't worry, but don't list them in the table.

Ascetic? or Active?

Name of Folklore Person	In chapter?	Ascetic	*Active*	Both
St. George	V		*x*	
St. Perpetua	IV			x
Rabbi Akiva	III	x		
Olaf Tryggvason	III			

Writing   Write about the characters from your table:

1. Put the ascetics in one paragraph. Be sure to give examples from the "r"eligious folktales showing how each was an ascetic.

2. Put the active people in another paragraph. Give examples from the tales for each of them.

3. Last, discuss those characters, with examples, who are both ascetic and active.

Chapter IX
Ages of Man

Introduction and Overview

An Important Topic in Religion

Religions have all been concerned with age.

- Some have explored the age of the earth; others have explored the age of history.

- Almost all have looked closely at the age of a human being: the life span of a man or a woman. This includes: what people look like at each stage, how they behave as they grow, etc.

In this chapter, you will explore how a number of "r"eligious folktales look at the life of a person. Then you will look at how a famous English bard wrote about the same topic.

What to do: Learning Objectives

➢ Compare and contrast a number of selections about the ages of man.

➢ Use a timeline to organize your writing about the selections.

➢ Using a timeline, develop your own ages of man.

Companion Guide

This workbook is a companion to *"Snipp snapp snute, så er eventyret ute" – Folklore Reader and Critical Thinking Workbook*, which has additional critical thinking materials and reading selections.

Continued on next page

Introduction and Overview, Continued

Chapter Components

A text or group of texts that you will read. Most of the writing and other work you do require you to read and refer to these text resource(s).

Any of a number of activities or exercises which you need to complete. These activities may include:

- Vocabulary exercises.
- Questions to answer.
- Study tables to complete
- Thinking organizers (graphic or picture diagrams) to fill out.
- Written work to plan, organize, and write.

All these activities should help you to read and understand the texts or to write about them. You may have to complete a project, which requires limited research.

Content

You are going to read the following selections:

- Aesop's fable: "The Man, the Horse, the Ox, and the Dog."

- "The Seven Stages of Life" by Rabbi Simon.

- "The Story of Man and His Years," a folktale from Romania.

- William Shakespeare's "The Ages of Man."

Aesop's Fable about the Ages of Man

One of the Earliest

The first "r"eligious folktale about the ages of man is from the ancient Greek fable-teller Aesop. You might say his is one of the earliest folktales about the age of man the human. Might it be the basis on which the other folktales about age are built? Read Aesop's fable.

"The Man, the Horse, the Ox, and the Dog"
Retold by V. S. Vernon Jones

One winter's day, during a severe storm, a horse, an ox, and a dog came and begged for shelter in the house of a man. He readily admitted them, and, as they were cold and wet, he lit a fire for their comfort. He [then] put oats before the horse and hay before the ox, while he fed the dog with the remains of his own dinner.

The storm abated [lessened]. As the [animals] were about to depart, they determined to show their gratitude in the following way: They divided the life of man among them, and each endowed [gave] one part of [the man's life] with the qualities which were peculiarly his own. [For example], the horse took youth. [In this part of a man's life], ... young men are high-mettled [high spirited] and impatient ... [with little] restraint [like horses].

The ox took middle age. ... Accordingly, men in middle life are steady and hard-working. ... The dog took old age, which is the reason why old men are so often peevish and ill-tempered. Like dogs, ... [old men are] attached chiefly to those who look to their comfort [take care of them, [but] ... they are disposed to snap at those who are unfamiliar or distasteful to them.

From: V. S. Vernon Jones. *Aesop's Fables.* New York: Doubleday, Page and Company, 1912. Not in copyright. At: http://www.archive.org/search.php?query=Aesop%27s%20Fables%20AND%20mediatype%3Atexts

Mini-exercise

Complete the study table that follows. Read the directions for the table.

Continued on next page

Aesop's Fable about the Ages of Man, Continued

So, how many ages did Aesop talk about?

- **List Aesop's ages of man in order below.**
- **Then give each a good title that describes it:**

What descriptive words are associated with each age your listed?

- **Write below each age you listed under Name of Age.**
- **Reread the fable.**
- **Then put, beside each age, a few descriptive words from the fable for each age under Descriptive Words.**

Name of Age	Descriptive Words

A Hebrew Viewpoint

Same?
Different?

Now, read a Hebrew version, called "The Seven Stages of Life. See how it is similar to and different from Aesop's fable.

"The Seven Stages of Life"
Rabbi Simon,
(translated by Hyman Hurwitz)

The first commences [starts] in the first year of human existence, when the infant lies like a king on a soft couch, with numerous attendants about him, all ready to serve him, and eager to testify their love and attachment by kisses and embraces.

The second commences about the age of two or three years, when the darling child is permitted to crawl on the ground and, like an unclean animal, delights in dirt and filth.

Then, at the age of ten, the thoughtless boy, without reflecting on the past or caring for the future, jumps and skips about like a young kid [goat] on the enameled green, contented to enjoy the present moment.

The fourth stage begins about the age of twenty, when the young man, full of vanity and pride, begins to set off his person by dress. … Like a young, unbroken horse, he prances and gallops about in search of a wife.

Then comes the matrimonial [married] state, when the poor man, like the patient ass [donkey], is obliged, how-ever reluctantly, to … [work] for a living.

Behold him now in the parental state, when, [he is] surrounded by helpless children craving his support, and looking to him for bread. He is as bold, … vigilant [watchful] and .. fawning [bowing], … as a faithful dog guarding his little flock [of sheep], and snatching at everything that comes in his way, in order to provide for his offspring.

At last comes the final stage, when the decrepit [weaken and broken] old man, like the unwieldy [heavy] though sagacious [wise] elephant, becomes grave, sedate [dignified], and distrustful. He then, also, begins to hang down his head toward the ground, as if surveying the place where all his vast schemes must terminate, and where ambition and vanity are finally humbled to the dust.

From: William Clouston. *Flowers from a Persian Garden and Other Paper*. London: D. Nutt, 1890. Not in copyright. At: http://ia331321.us.archive.org/1/items/flowersfromapers16949gut/16949-8.txt

Continued on next page

A Hebrew Viewpoint, Continued

Mini-exercise   Complete the study table below. Follow the directions in the table.

Review "The Seven Stages of Life." **Below give a name to each stage if there wasn't one in the excerpt. Then write a summary of each stage in your own words.**

Stage No.	Name of Stage	Descriptive Summary
I.		
II.		
III.		
IV.		
V.		
VI.		
VII.		

A Romanian Version

What about this one? Now read "The Story of Man and His Years," a folktale from Romania. How is it similar to and different from the two earlier tales you read.

"CXVI. The Story of Man and His Years"
Moses Gaster
(From Romania)

When God had created the world, he called all his creatures together to grant them their span of life, and to tell them how long they would live and what manner of life they would lead.

The first to appear before God was man. And God said to him, "Thou, man, shall be king of the world, walking erect upon thy feet and looking up to heaven. I give thee a noble countenance [physical body]; the power of thought and judgment shall be thine [yours], and the capacity of disclosing thy innermost thoughts by means of speech [i.e., man can talk]. All that lives and moves and goes about the earth shall be under thy rule, the winged birds and the creeping things shall obey thee, thine [yours] shall be all the fruits of the tree and land, and thy [your] life shall be thirty years."

Then man turned away dissatisfied and grumbling: "What is the good of living in pleasure and in might, if all [my] years … are to be thirty only?" So did man speak and grumble, especially when he heard … the years granted to other animals.

The turn came to the ass [donkey]. He stepped forward to hear what God had decreed for him. The Creator said, "You shall work hard ; you shall carry heavy burdens and be constantly beaten. You shall always be scolded and have very little rest, your food shall be a poor one of thistles and thorns, and your life shall be fifty years."

When the ass heard what God had decreed for him, he fell upon his knees and cried, "All merciful Creator, am I to lead such a miserable life, and am I to have such poor food as thistles and thorns. Am I to work so hard and carry such heavy burdens and then live on for fifty years in such misery? Have pity on me and take off twenty years."

Then man, greedy … [for] a long life, stepped forward and begged for himself these twenty years which the donkey had rejected. The Lord granted them to him.

Then came the dog. To him, the Creator said, "You shall guard the house and the property of your master ; you shall cling to them as if your were afraid of losing them; you shall bark even at the shadow of the moon, and for all your trouble you shall gnaw bones and eat raw meat, and your life shall be forty years."

"All merciful Creator," cried the dog, " if my life is to be full of worry and trouble, and if I am to live on bones and raw stuff, take off, please, twenty years."

Again [greedy] man … stepped forward and begged the Creator to give him the twenty years rejected by the dog. And the Creator again granted man's request.

Think about: What are the differences between this folktale and Aesop's fable?

Continued on next page

A Romanian Version, Continued

Now, it was the turn of the monkey. The Creator said, "You shall only have the likeness of man, but not be man; you shall be stupid and childish. Your back shall be bent; you shall be an object of mockery to the children and a laughing-stock of fools, and your life shall be sixty years."

When the monkey heard what was decreed for him, he fell upon his knees and said, "All merciful God, in thy wisdom you have decided that I should be a man and not a man, that my back shall be bent, that I shall be a laughing-stock for young and fools and I shall be stupid. Take, in mercy, thirty years off my life." ... God, the all merciful, granted his request.

And again, man, whose greed can never be satisfied, stepped forward and asked also for these thirty years which the monkey had rejected. ... Again, God gave them to him.

Then God dismissed all the animals and all his creatures, and each one went to his appointed station and to the life that has been granted to him.

And as man has asked, so has it come to pass. Man lives as a king and ruler over all creatures for the thirty years, which the Lord had given to him, in joy and in happiness, without care and without trouble.

Then come the years from thirty to fifty, which are the years of the donkey; they are full of hard work, heavy burdens, and little food, for man is anxious to gather and to lay up something for the years to come. It could not be otherwise, for were not these the years which he had taken over from the ass?

Then come the years from fifty to seventy, when man sits at home and guards, with great trembling and fear, the little that he possesses, fearful of every shadow, eating little, always keeping others away lest they rob him of what he has gathered. He barks at every one whom he suspects of wanting to take away what belongs to him. ... No wonder that he behaves like that, for these are the dog's years, which man had asked for himself.

And if a man lives beyond seventy, then his back gets bent, his face changes, his mind gets clouded, he becomes childish, a laughing-stock for children, an amusement for the fool. These are the years which man had taken over from the monkey.

From: Moses Gaster. *Rumanian bird and beast stories*. London: Sidgwick and Jackson, 1915. Not in copyright. At: http://www.archive.org/stream/rumanianbirdbeas00gastuoft/rumanianbirdbeas00gastuoft_djvu.txt

---

Which are most similar?

Which two?   Clearly, two of these "r"eligious folktales are more closely related to each other. The third one is a little different.

You are going to:

> Write about the similarities between the two more closely related folktales.
> Tell how these two are different from the third tale.

To help you organize your writing, look at **Tips** below before you begin.

Writing

> In the first paragraph, introduce the three folktales by title. Give a bit about where they are from, how old you think they are, etc.

> In the second paragraph, write about the two "r"eligious folktales that are more closely related. Support you ideas about their strong similarities by giving examples from both tales.

> In the last paragraph, explain how the third tale is the "odd man out." It is different from the other two. You will need to show these differences by examples from the folktales.

Shakespeare's Stages of Man

Famous!   William Shakespeare used the seven ages in his play *As You Like It*. Read his interpretation of the stages in a person's life. Use the vocabulary below to help you with unfamiliar words:

Vocabulary to help you with the excerpt

bubble reputation = fame that is only temporary	**woeful** = sad and melancholy
of formal cut = carefully cut and trimmed	**spectacles** = eyeglasses (an old word)
mewling = crying and bawling	**capon** = a roasted chicken. The judge has been bribed with a chicken.

Continued on next page

Shakespeare's Stages of Man, Continued

All the world's a stage,
And all the men and women merely players [actors],
They have their exits and entrances,
And one man in his time plays many parts,

His [a man's] acts being seven ages [periods of life]. At first the infant,
Mewling and puking [throwing up] in the nurse's arms.
Then, the whining schoolboy with his satchel [little school bag]
And shining morning face, creeping like snail
Unwillingly to school. And then the lover,
Sighing like furnace, with a woeful ballad
Made to his mistress' eyebrow. Then a soldier,
Full of strange oaths, and bearded like the pard [leopard],
Jealous in honour, sudden, and quick in quarrel,
Seeking the bubble reputation
Even in the cannon's mouth [in war]. And then the justice [judge]
In fair round belly, with good capon lin'd,
With eyes severe [stern], and beard of formal cut,
Full of wise saws [sayings], and modern instances [examples],
And so he plays his part. The sixth age shifts
Into the lean and slipper'd pantaloon [a foolish old comical man],
With spectacles on nose, and pouch [a case for tobacco] on side,
His youthful hose [socks and pants] well sav'd, a world too wide,
For his shrunk shank [thigh or leg], and his big manly voice,
Turning again towards childish treble [high-pitch], pipes
And whistles in his sound. Last scene of all,
That ends this strange eventful history,
Is second childishness and mere oblivion [forgetfulness],
Sans [without] teeth, sans eyes, sans taste, sans everything.

From: *As You Like It:* Act II, Scene VII, lines 139-166. At:
http://en.wikipedia.org/wiki/All_the_world%27s_a_stage

Definition   This excerpt about the seven ages of man is called a monologue: This
means one person talks continuously about the subject. Often, the actor
may be alone on the stage or talking as though he is telling only the
audience his personal thoughts.

Continued on next page

Shakespeare's Ages of Man, Continued

Mini-exercise   Complete the tables. Follow the instructions in each table.

Below are the introductory lines to Shakespeare's monologue about the seven stages of man:

"All the world's a stage,
And all the men and women merely players,
They have their exits and entrances,"

Shakespeare is comparing the world to _____ and he is comparing men and women to _____

(Select only **one** letter.)

a.	exits … entrances.
b.	the universe … stars in the universe.
c.	a stage … players on that stage.
d.	Players … authors of plays.

"And one man in his time plays many parts,
His acts being seven ages. …"

The main theme in these lines is that _____

(Select only **one** letter.)

a.	women have no part in the ages.
b.	life of a person goes through a set number of stages.
c.	life is a journey, which has no plan.
d.	old age and youth are identical.

Timeline for Shakespeare's Excerpt

What to do   On the next page is a partially completed **Timeline** with the seven ages from Shakespeare's monologue.

Based on the excerpt:

➢ Give a name to each age and fill in the box with the person who represents that age.
➢ Then add a couple of traits beside the person.

We have started the timeline; you finish it.

Continued on next page

Timeline for Shakespeare's "The Seven Ages of Man"

Age 1 Name	Stage 1 Person
Infancy (Baby)	*Baby — bawling, crying*

↓

Age 2 Name	Stage 2 Person
Childhood	

↓

Age 3 Name	Stage 3 Person

↓

Age 4 Name	Stage 4 Person
Manhood	

↓

Age 5 Name	Stage 5 Person
	Justice

↓

Age 6 Name	Stage 6 Person
Retirement	

↓

Age 7 Name	Stage 7 Person

Your Ages of Man/Woman

What to do

You have read a number of examples of the stages or ages in a person's life from "r"eligious folktales and from Shakespeare.

Using the **Timeline** that follows, plan out your seven, eight, however many, ages you want in your idea of the stages in a person's life.

> ➤ You can use either a man or woman for you timeline.
>
> ➤ You can make this project serious or you can make it comical. Think about your attitude and approach to your ages of life.
>
> ➤ As you write the person in the timeline, add a couple of descriptive words about the person. This will help you write about your own ages.

We have filled in the first age and have left space for seven stages. If you need more, use **For Notes about your timeline**. It follows the table on the next page.

Continued on next page

Timeline for Your "Ages of Man/Woman"

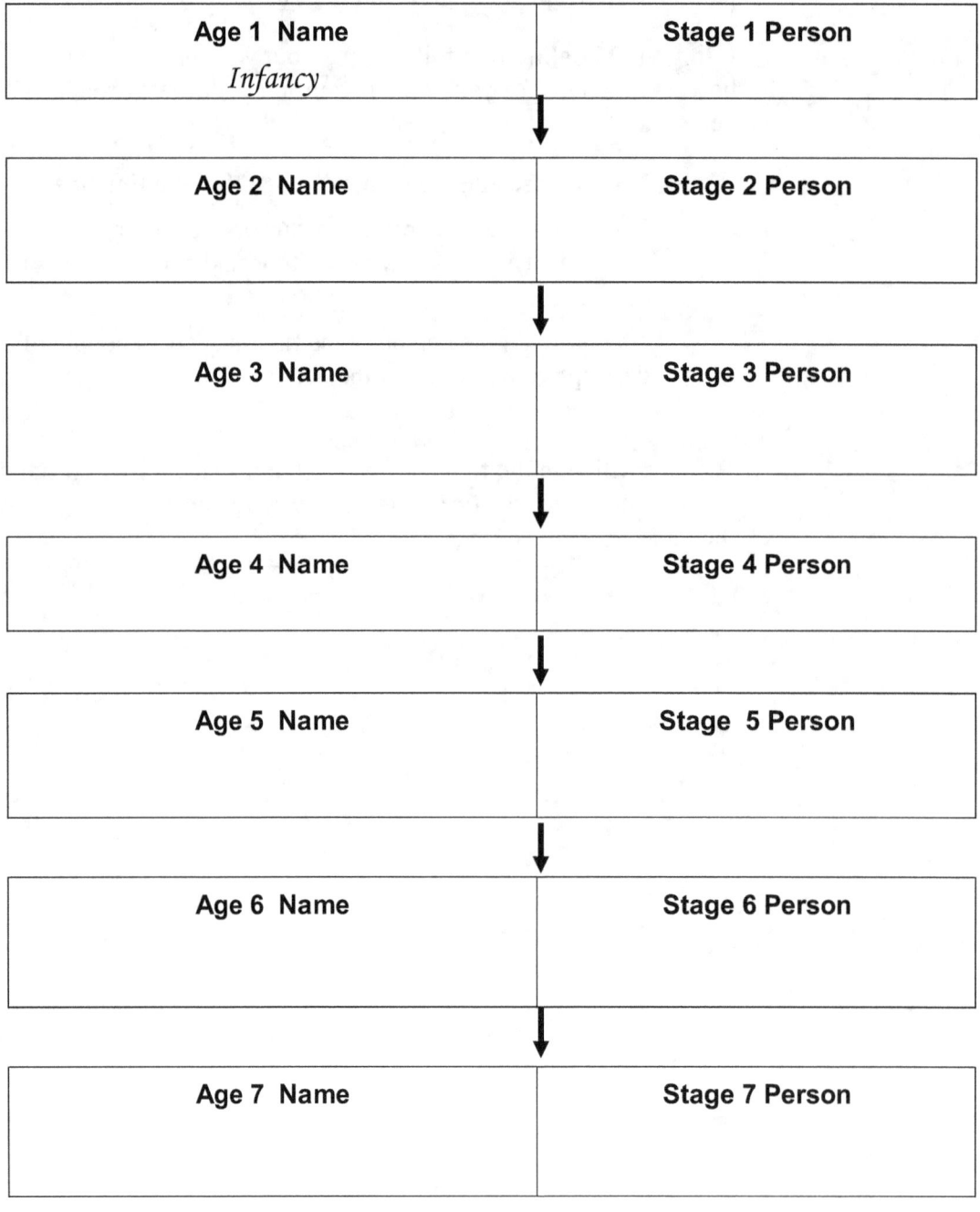

Age 1 Name	Stage 1 Person
Infancy	

Age 2 Name	Stage 2 Person

Age 3 Name	Stage 3 Person

Age 4 Name	Stage 4 Person

Age 5 Name	Stage 5 Person

Age 6 Name	Stage 6 Person

Age 7 Name	Stage 7 Person

Write about your ages of man/woman

What to do   Now, using the **Timeline for Your "Ages of Man/Woman,"** which you have just completed, write about each of your ages:

> ➢ Keep each age in a separate paragraph.
>
> ➢ Be sure to name the age.
>
> ➢ Include the kinds of people in each age.
>
> ➢ Give some kind of description of the age as well as the people in that age.

Remember, you can be serious or comical about this writing, but be consistent in your approach.

A Final View from Hinduism: The *Ashrams* of Life

The first ashram or stage of life , _Brahmacharya_, is the student phase of life when the person is supposed to immerse himself or herself in learning the craft or trade in preparation for later life. During this period the person is supposed to live a celibate life (_Brahmacharya_ means celibacy, unmarried).

Grahasta (meaning "householder") ashram is the stage of family life. It begins with marriage and leads to raising a family. It involves earning a living through the skills acquired during _Brahmacharya_ ashram. The householders have the responsibility of bringing up their children in the same way that their parents brought them up. The householder needs to perform his religious duties as well.

Vanaprastha, the next stage indicates the departure from material possessions. The person lives with the family, in society, but in a withdrawn manner. The man no longer takes part in the commercial activities, and the woman leaves the running of the household to her daughter-in-law. People in this ashram play the role of mentors. …

The final stage is _Sanyasa_ or renunciation. The person leaves or renounces society to spend the remainder of his or her life in meditation and the contemplation of God in solitude.

Adapted from: http://hinduism.suite101.com/article.cfm/the_four_ashrams_or_life_stages

Think about: So what do you think of this Hindu version of the stages of life, from India? How is it similar to and different from the other excerpts you have read? What does this version emphasize that the other versions do not?

For your notes

Chapter X
An Insect or Two

Introduction and Overview

Spiders ?

Proverbs XXX: 28 -- The spider "takes hold with her hands and is considered …one of the four small creatures which are very little but very smart.

Job VIII:14 -- "Their confidence hangs by a thread. They are relying on a spider's web. (Adapted from *New Living Translation* 2007.)

Quran 29:41 -- "… but verily, the frailest (weakest) of houses is the spider's house - if they knew."

From an Apache creation folk myth – "Tarantula spun a black cord and, attaching it to the brown ball, crawled away fast to the east, pulling on the cord with all his strength. Tarantula … did the same with a blue cord to the south, a yellow cord to the west, and a white cord to the north. With mighty pulls in each direction, the brown ball stretched to immeasurable size -- it became the earth!"

(Adapted from: http://www.care2.com/c2c/groups/disc.html?gpp=4011&pst=175248)

As you can see, this little insect plays an important part in many religions. In some cases, it teaches a moral lesson; in others, it is the basis for explanations about how things came to be. There are even stories about tricky spiders which helped man.

You are going to read about how spiders helped a number of holy people.

What to do: Learning Objectives

➤ Compare and contrast a number of "r"eligious folktales about insects.

➤ Use an organizer to sort the elements of each tale, based on your own attributes/traits.

➤ Write about the similarities and differences of any three of the insect folktales.

Continued on next page

Introduction and Overview, Continued

Companion Guide

This workbook is a companion to *"Snipp snapp snute, så er eventyret ute" – Folklore Reader and Critical Thinking Workbook*, which has additional critical thinking materials and reading selections.

Chapter Components

A text or group of texts that you will read. Most of the writing and other work you do require you to read and refer to these text resource(s). There are also any number of activities or exercises which you need to complete. These activities may include:

- Vocabulary exercises.
- Questions to answer.
- Study tables to complete
- Thinking organizers (graphic or picture diagrams) to fill out.
- Written work to plan, organize, and write.

All these activities should help you to read and understand the texts or to write about them. You may have to complete a project, which requires limited research.

Content

You are going to read the following selections:

- Muhammad and the Spider.

- David and the Spider.

- Yorimoto and his Spider.

- "St. Felix and the Spider."

Some Spider Folktales

Muhammad's Spider
The following incident occurred when Prophet Muhammad was being chased by his enemies near Mecca.

Muhammad and the Spider

Once as his enemies were catching up with him, Muhammad hid in a deep cave. Crouching far in a dark corner, he prayed, "Allah, protect and save me from your enemies."

Suddenly the entrance to the cave darkened. "They have arrived," thought Muhammad, ready to draw his sword. "What's this?," he said to himself, looking at the entrance again. "A tree – in front of the cave?"

In truth, an acacia tree had sprouted and grown up right at the entrance to the cave. Then he saw a wood-pigeon fly down and start to build a nest in the tree. Muhammad stood amazed.

Finally, the pagan warriors from Mecca arrived. Muhammad could hear their cries as they search around the outside of the cave. As they were about to enter the cave, one of them said in a commanding voice:

> **"Look there's no point in searching in that cave. Don't you see, that bird has built a nest there. She has been nesting for a while. And look, there is a wide spider web hanging from the tree to the cave entrance. If there were someone in the cave, he would have broken and damaged the spider web when he went in."**

The group of enemy soldiers then left. Muhammad gave a sign of relief and thanked Allah for his protection.

Adapted from: http://australianmuseum.net.au/Spiders-in-history

---

David and the Spider
Now, read about how David escaped from King Saul and his soldiers. Look for similarities to and difference from the folktale about Muhammad.

Continued on next page

Some Spider Folktales, Continued

David and the Spider

David, the shepherd, was being pursued by King Saul. In panic, he came to a cave.

"In I go," David said to himself. "And may Jehovah protect me."

Then David hid as far back in the cave as he could, squeezing himself into a little hump. Saul's warriors arrived soon after. Through the clatter of arms and the tramping of feet, David heard Saul's voice yelling: "Have you found him? He can't be far away."

"Sire," replied one of his commanders, "there is a cave here. Would your majesty come and see." David heard a scuffing sound like someone shoving.

"No need to search in that cave," came Saul's voice. "That spider web covering the doorway has been there for quite a while. If that little shepherd had gone into the cave, he would have snapped the web and broken it. Can't you see it is still whole and untouched! Tell the troops to look over the hill."

When Saul and his troops had left, David left the cave, thanking the Lord for His protection.

Adapted from: http://australianmuseum.net.au/Spiders-in-history

---

A Japanese Spider Tale

Here is a similar spider tale from Japan. It is about Yorimoto, a warrior who tried to lead a rebellion against the Taira's, the ruling family in Japan.

Continued on next page

Some Spider Folktales, Continued

Yorimoto and his Spider

Yorimoto, the warrior, had been outnumbered and was now on the run. "Up the mountain to the forest," he thought, as he stumbled up the rocky slope. "I can hide in the forest, under some log or deep in some bushes."

Yorimoto pushed through the scratching branches into the forest. "Where to go?" he thought. One tree was too old; it would fall if he climbed it. Another tree didn't have enough leaves to hide him. Then up ahead, he saw an old thick tree with a broad trunk. Up on the trunk was a hole.

"I wonder," thought Yorimoto, "if I could fit into that hole." He shinnied up the tree as if it were a smooth pole. "Ah," he said, "like an owl in its home," as he pushed himself into the hole. He kept himself as far back in the tree hollow as he could, away from the light.

He waited and watched. Then he noticed that the light coming into the hollow was getting shaded as though a cloud were passing in front of the sun and blocking the light. Only Yorimoto couldn't see a cloud in the sky. "Ah," he said. "It is a spider. The little fellow is making a web in front of the hollow." As he continued to watch, the little spider completely covered the entrance to the hollow with its web.

After a while, he heard voices below. "He has to be up in a tree," said a deep voice.

"Do you think, your honor that he could hide in such thin trees. It will be too easy to see him if he has," answered a thin voice.

"A hollow – hole, there on that tree," came a third husky voice. "Your honor, should we send someone up to look inside." The command was given. Yorimoto heard a scratching and scraping as some soldier climbed. He huddled farther back in the hollow. The soldier's head appeared outside the hole. Then he stopped.

"Your honor, the hole has been sealed by a spider web. No one could get inside the hollow without disturbing the web, and it is perfect – unbroken."

"Come down," replied the deep voice, and the soldier's head disappeared. Yorimoto heard the command to move on and the tramping of departing boots. You can believe he gave a sigh of relief as he began to descend from the tree.

Adapted from: http://australianmuseum.net.au/Spiders-in-history

---

A Saint's Spider

This last tale is about a saint who was escaping from a Roman emperor's soldiers.

Continued on next page

Some Spider Folktales, Continued

"St. Felix and the Spider"

In the 3rd century CE, the pagan Roman emperor Decius persecuted the Christians mightily [very much]. One of the holy men he was determined to capture and kill was St. Felix from Syria. Decius sent troops to Nola, St. Felix' hometown.

As he left … one day to seek a place of safety, Felix came face to face with the very men who were searching for him to take his life. They did not, however, know who Felix was, and, waylaying [stopping] him, asked: "Have you met one Felix on your way?"

"Nay [no]," answered Felix, "I haven't seen him." Then both he and the soldiers hurried away, in opposite directions. Felix, knowing that it was only a matter of minutes before the searchers should learn his identity and rush after him, fled toward the edge of the town.

There, Felix came to a ruined wall whose face was cleft [split] with a narrow rift [slit]. He crept with difficulty through this rift and found among the ruins beyond the wall a dry well … He hid himself in the well. The soldiers, not finding him in his house and now knowing his face and the clothing he had been wearing, … [hurried back] … , expecting to find St. Felix still on the road.

The soldiers came to the wall with the cleft. St. Felix could hear their voices, and his heart stood still as he heard one soldier suggest searching beyond the wall.

"Nay," answered another, "it would be useless to look beyond this narrow opening. Don't you see? No man has passed through in many a day, for I have never seen such a heavy spider web. A web like this … [took a lot of time]! It is heavy as grey armor."

With that, the soldiers departed, leaving Felix safe and secure behind the spider web.

Adapted from: "Felix of Nola" at http://en.wikipedia.org/wiki/Felix_of_Nola and from: The Baldwin Project: "St. Felix and the Spider" at http://www.mainlesson.com/display.php?author=hallg&book=saints&story=felix

Compare and contrast the spider folktales

Preparing

Reread the folktales. Then choose any **three** of them to compare and contrast. Read **Tips for Comparing** on the next page to help organize your thinking.

Continue on next page

Compare and contrast the spider folktales, Continued

Tips for Comparing

➢ In the **Topic Sentences** table below, write a sentence about each area or topic where the three folktales your chose are completely similar. We have filled in one sentence for you.

➢ Remember, each of these sentences will become the topic sentence of a short paragraph.

➢ Take your examples for supporting each topic sentence directly from the story.

Topic Sentences for Similarities in the Spider Folktales

1.	All three tales are about the same insect.
2.	
3.	
4.	
5.	
6.	
7.	
8.	
9.	
10.	

Continued on next page

Compare and contrast the spider folktales, Continued

Tips for Contrasting

➤ Use the **Contrast Table** below to help you sort out the differences between the three tales you chose.

> ➤ **In the second column, write the Title of your first tale.**
>
> ➤ **In the third column, write the Title of your second tale.**
>
> ➤ **In the fourth column, write the Title of your third tale.**

➤ Under the first column, called **Trait or Attribute**, write the general topic that is different in the tales. A number of examples might be: A tree, a well, type of pursuers, etc. These are a few of the general differences that you could use, depending on the tales which you chose.

➤ Now put an **X** in under any title where the **Trait or Attribute** occurs in the tale. Do **not** put an "X" if the trait is not in a tale.

Contrast Table for the three Spider Tales

Trait or Attribute	Title of your first tale:	Title of your second tale:	Title of your third tale:
Each hero is a different nationality.	X	X	X

Write about the similarities and differences in the spider tales

Tips for Writing

In writing your comparison,

> ➤ Make each sentence which you wrote in **Topic Sentences for Similarities in the Spider Folktales** a topic sentence.

> ➤ Fill examples in from the actual folktales to support each topic sentence.

In writing your contrast,

> ➤ Write each attribute from the **Contrast Table** as part of a topic sentence.

> ➤ Then to support the difference, write an example from the folktale or tales where you found it. These examples should support the contrasting attribute in your topic sentence.

For your notes

Chapter XI
The Journey Unending

Introduction and Overview

Definition

All holy folk in religions worldwide have blessed their followers. Each prophet or leader has often performed what holy writings call miracles. These might be healing the ill, curing the insane, even resurrecting people from death.

"R"eligious folklore is also filled with a contrast to these blessings.

- In this case, Muhammad or Jesus or another religious leader imposed eternal wandering on a person.

- In some instances, tthe person had to live with this endless journey.

In this chapter, you will explore some of the people who were forced to wander eternally.

What to do:
Learning
Objectives

➤ Contrast "The Wandering Jew" (from England) with "The Shoemaker of Jerusalem" (from Norway).
➤ Find implicit and explicit in two poems about the Wandering Jew.
➤ Analyze the Wandering Jew's feelings in Riley's poem "The Wandering Jew."
➤ Develop a composite character sketch of the Wandering Jew from three reading selections in this chapter.

Companion
Guide

This workbook is a companion to *"Snipp snapp snute, så er eventyret ute" – Folklore Reader and Critical Thinking Workbook*, which has additional critical thinking materials and reading selections.

Continued on next page

Introduction and Overview, Continued

Chapter Components

A text or group of texts that you will read. Most of the writing and other work you do require you to read and refer to these text resource(s).
Any of a number of activities or exercises which you need to complete. These activities may include:

- Vocabulary exercises.
- Questions to answer.
- Study tables to complete
- Thinking organizers (graphic or picture diagrams) to fill out.
- Written work to plan, organize, and write.

All these activities should help you to read and understand the texts or to write about them. You may have to complete a project, which requires limited research.

Content: Selections

The selections in this chapter include:

- "The Wandering Jew" (from England)

- "The Shoemaker of Jerusalem" (from Norway)

- "Song for the Wandering Jew" by William Wordsworth

- "The Wandering Jew" by James Whitcomb Riley

Eternal Wanderer

A Very Famous Figure This person is perhaps the most famous "r"eligious folklore "hero." He is known throughout the world. He has been celebrated in poetry, drama, and fiction. One famous Nobel prize writer, Per Lagerkvist, wrote a novel about him.

"The Wandering Jew"
(An English Version)

The story of the Wandering Jew is [very old] …. In 1228 CE, [supposedly] … an Armenian archbishop [came to] … England, to visit the shrines and relics [Saint's bones] preserved in English churches, … He was welcomed at St. Alban's monastery. … While staying there, a monk asked him … if he had ever seen or heard of the famous person name Joseph, who was present at the crucifixion and conversed with Jesus. … The Armenian archbishop replied that he had met the man. He then said that Joseph was originally a [guard] of Pontius Pilate [who had condemned Jesus to be crucified]. At that time he was not Christian and was named Cartaphilus As the Romans were dragging Jesus out the door to take him to Golgotha, Cartaphilus had yelled at Jesus: "Go faster, Jesus, go faster: Why do you linger?"

Jesus looked at Cartaphilus with a frown, and said, "I indeed am going, but you shall wait until I come [return]." Soon after, Cartaphilus was converted to Christianity and baptized with the name of Joseph.

Joseph lives on forever. At the end of every hundred years he gets an incurable illness. When he recovers, he returns to the same state of youth, about age 30, he was in when Jesus suffered. Joseph remembers all the circumstances of the death and resurrection of Christ, the saints that arose with him, the composing of the apostles' creed, their preaching, and dispersion … . He is a very grave [serious] and holy person. This is the substance of the Armenian archbishop's story of Joseph's eternal wandering.

> Adapted from: Thomas Percy. *Percy's Reliques of Ancient English Poetry*: Volume II. London: J. M Dent and Company, 1889. Pp. 21-26. Not in copyright. At: http://www.archive.org/details/percysreliquesof02percuoft

---

Mini-exercise Complete the study tables. Follow the directions in each table.

Continued on next page

Eternal Wanderer, Continued

The Armenian archbishop told this story in England in _____

(Circle **only one letter**.)

a.	1730 CE.
b.	1557 CE.
c.	1228 CE.
d.	33 CE.

The story about Joseph and Christ took place about _____

(Circle **one** letter.)

a.	1500 CE.
b.	1230 CE.
c.	1228 CE.
d.	33 CE.

Joseph's pagan name was _____

(Circle **only the letter** that applies.)

a.	Pilate.
b.	Simon.
c.	Cartaphilus.
d.	Artaban.

What was the curse that Joseph had to endure? Explain.
(Write your answer below.)

Continued on next page

The Shoemaker of Jerusalem

Another Version

Here is a second version of the famous eternal wanderer. As you read, note the differences between this version and the one from England.

"The Shoemaker of Jerusalem"
(A Norwegian Version)

At that time Jesus was carrying the cross, He wanted to stop and rest a bit by the house of the shoemaker named Ahasverus, but He wasn't allowed to because Ahasverus hit Jesus in the face. So as a punishment for this, the shoemaker was made to wander round the world in the clothes he had on, without food or drink and with his shoemaker's awl on his back.

About a hundred years ago, Eli Bjørnstad saw the shoemaker one morning on the wooden step bridge. He was sitting there and resting. He was so terrible to look at: He had only rags on. His grimy face was all overgrown with white hair and a beard. He had his cobbler's awl on his back, and it was all green with moss. However when he caught sight of Eli, he went fast away from her eyes. This wandering Jew was later seen in Nordre Haga, where he was sitting on a stone by the bridge.

There is folk song about him; one of the verses goes this way:

> A shoemaker have I been
> in Jerusalem living;
> Christ have I dishonored
> and cursed him mightily;
> I took no pity on
> his [Jesus'] innocent blood,
> Therefore must I wander round
> as punishment -- a mirror for all

From: Lars M. Fjellstad. Norsk Folkeminnelags Skrifter. (Internt referansenummer: 23.03.09 – A. Oslo: Folkeminne frå Eidskog III Norsk Folkeminnelag Nr. 98, Universitetsforlaget. At: http://www.historier.no/index.php?option=com_sobi2&sobi2Task=sobi2Details&catid=509&sobi2Id=5689&Itemid=305. (Translated and adapted by David Garnett.)

Continued on next page

Contrast the Wandering Jew with the shoemaker

Contrast

You are going to contrast or show the differences between the two the Wandering Jew and the Shoemaker of Jerusalem.

> ➢ We have started the contrast table for you. You complete it.

> ➢ There is a couple of blanks under *Trait or Attribute* for you to fill in if a trait or attribute has been left off the table.

> ➢ You will need to go back and read the stories carefully. Remember to use your own words.

Contrast Table

How the Wandering Jew showed the trait	*Trait or Attribute*	How the Shoemaker showed the trait
Guard of Pilate	*Job or Position in Society*	Poor shoemaker
	What Jesus did	
	What he did to Jesus	
	What Jesus said to each man	
At Pilate's judgment	*Where it happened*	
Like a holy man	*How person looked*	
Became a Christian	*Change in person?*	
	Where the story was told	Norway
	Who told the story	

Writing

Now write about the differences between "The Wandering Jew" from England and "The Shoemaker of Jerusalem" from Norway. Read **Tips** before you start your writing.

Continued on next page

Contrast the Wandering Jew with the shoemaker,
Continued

Tips
- Write three or four paragraphs about the differences.

- Include one item under *Trait or Attribute* in your topic sentence. Each of the items is general point that makes a difference.

- To support the difference in each topic sentence, use the items on either side of the trait or attribute as supporting sentence in your paragraph.

- Do the same thing for the next item under *Trait or Attribute*. Continue on in the same way until you finish your writing.

Two Poems about the Wandering Jew

Purpose
You are going to read two poems about the Wandering Jew. The important points to look for in these two poems is not a description of the Wandering Jew, but how he feels and thinks.

After you read these two poems, you will build a character sketch of the Wandering Jew from them. This will mean looking at

- What is explicit or stated in the poems.

- What is implicit or not directly stated.

Your character sketch of the Wandering Jew will include both of these.

Two Poems about the Wandering Jew, Continued

"Song for the Wandering Jew"
William Wordsworth (not in copyright)

Though the torrents from their fountains
Roar down many a craggy steep,
Yet they find among the mountains
Resting-places calm and deep.

Clouds that love through air to hasten,
Ere the storm its fury stills,
Helmet-like themselves will fasten
On the heads of towering hills.

What, if through the frozen centre
Of the Alps the Chamois [mountain leopard] bound,
Yet he has a home to enter
In some nook [corner] of chosen ground:

And the Sea-horse, though the ocean
Yield him no domestic cave,
Slumbers without sense of motion,
Couched upon the rocking wave.

If on windy days the Raven
Gambol like a dancing skiff,
Not the less she loves her haven
In the bosom of the cliff.

The fleet Ostrich, till day closes,
Vagrant over desert sands,
Brooding on her eggs reposes
When chill night that care demands.

Day and night my toils [hard tasks] redouble,
Never nearer to the goal;
Night and day, I feel the trouble
Of the Wanderer in my soul.

Continued on next page

Two Poems about the Wandering Jew, Continued

Mini-exercise   Complete the study tables. Follow the directions in each table.

Matching	
Draw a line from the nature phenomenon or animal in **Column A** to the place where it belongs or lives in **Column B**.	
Column A **Phenomena**	**Column B** **Places**
"fleet ostrich"	"on a rocking wave."
"sea-horse"	"on the heads of towering hills."
chamois	"the bosom of the cliff.".
clouds	Her nest with eggs.
raven	"A nook of chosen ground".

Explain the basic difference **between the Wandering Jew and all the nature phenomena and animals in Wordsworth's poem.**   (Write your answer below.)

Continued on next page

Two Poems about the Wandering Jew, Continued

A Second Poem   As you read this second poem about the Wandering Jew by the American poet, James Whitcomb Riley, try to look at the wanderer's thoughts and feelings as you did in the earlier poem by Wordsworth.

The vocabulary below should help you with unfamiliar words:

Tempest = a strong, violent storm
Clime = place
Quest = search
Brink = the edge
Distressed = unnerved
Dusky = somewhat dark in color, swarthy
Fain = would willingly, would like
Kine = cattle, primarily milk cows
Couch = lie down
Fetid = stinking
Unscathed = not touched or not affected
As 'twere a jest = as if it were joking with me

"The Wandering Jew"
James Whitcomb Riley (not in copyright)

The stars are falling, and the sky   *What kind of feeling does nature give?*
Is like a field of faded flowers;
The winds on weary wings go by;
The moon hides, and the tempest lowers;
And still through every clime and age
I wander on a pilgrimage
That all men know an idle quest,
For that the goal I seek is - Rest!   *What does the wanderer seek?*

I hear the voice of summer streams,
And following, I find the brink
Of cooling springs, with childish dreams
Returning as I bend to drink -
But suddenly, with startled eyes,
My face looks on its grim disguise
Of long gray beard; and so, distressed,
I hasten on, nor taste of rest.   *Why does the wanderer run away?*

Continued on next page

Two Poems about the Wandering Jew, Continued

I come upon a merry group
Of children in the dusky wood,
Who answer back the owlet's whoop,
That laughs as it had understood;
And I would pause a little space,
But that each happy blossom-face
Is like to one His hands have blessed
Who sent me forth in search of rest. *Whom do these children remind the wanderer of?*

Sometimes I fain would stay [stop] my feet
In shady lanes, where huddled kine
Couch in the grasses cool and sweet,
And lift their patient eyes to mine;
But I, for thoughts that ever then
Go back to Bethlehem again, *What do the cattle make the wanderer think of?*
Must needs fare [continue to travel] on my weary quest,
And weep for very need of rest.

Is there no end? I plead in vain:
Lost worlds nor living answer me. *When did the wanderer begin his wandering?*
Since Pontius Pilate's awful reign
Have I not passed eternity?
Have I not drunk the fetid breath
Of every fevered phase of death, *What happens to the wanderer when he gets ill?*
And come unscathed through every pest
And scourge and plague that promised rest?

Have I not seen the stars go out
That shed their light o'er Galilee, *Why might the stars go out over Galilee?*
And mighty kingdoms tossed about
And crumbled clod-like in the sea?
Dead ashes of dead ages blow
And cover me like drifting snow,
And time laughs on as 'twere a jest *What is the wanderer's "enemy"? Why?*
That I have any need of rest.

Continued on next page

Look at the Wandering Jew's feelings in the poem

Two Kinds of Feeling

- Some parts of James Whitcomb Riley's poem are filled with peace and happiness. You get a sense of contentment.

- Other parts are gloomy and sad. In these, you get a sense of unhappiness, even longing.

➤ You are going to sort the poem into these two categories and then write about them.

➤ To help you, do **Sort for Feelings** on the next page. Read Tips below to help you use the table.

Tips

Look at each quotation in **Quotations from the Poem**.

➤ Decide if the quotation expresses

- feelings of happiness and peace

    or

- feelings of sadness and despair.

➤ Mark either *Joy and Peace* or **Sadness and Gloom** for each quotation. Remember, you can **only** mark one block for each quotation.

There are some blanks under **Quotations from the Poem**. You can fill in and mark other quotations from the poem that you feel are important.

Sort for Riley's "The Wandering Jew"

Sort for the Wandering Jew's Feelings

Quotations from the Poem	*Joy and Peace*	Sadness and Gloom
"The stars are falling"		X
""The winds on weary wings …"		
"The moon hides …"		
" … an idle quest …"		X
"cooling springs"	X	
""distressed …"		
" … merry group of children …"	X	
"each happy blossom face …"		
"huddled kine … on grasses … sweet"		
"weary quest … in search of rest"		
"Is there no end?"		X
"… in vain"		
"fetid breath of … death"		
"ashes of dead ages … cover me"		

Summarize the Wandering Jew's feelings

Writing

Now that you have completed the sort table, write at least two paragraphs about the Wandering Jew's feelings in Riley's poem:

➢ At least one paragraph should be about the joy and peace in the poem. Be sure to express how the Wandering Jew reacts to these happy scenes.

➢ A second paragraph should cover the sadness and gloom in the poem. Again, include how the Wandering Jew reacts to these unhappy scenes.

The quotations in the table can easily support your topic sentences, which you could get from the titles of the checked columns.

Develop a composite character sketch of the Wandering Jew/ the shoemaker

What you will do

➢ In this section, you will do a character sketch of Ahasverus, building his character from the following selections:

- "The Wandering Jew" by James Whitcomb Riley
- "Song for the Wandering Jew" by William Wordsworth
- "The Shoemaker of Jerusalem" (from Norway)

➢ You are going to try to figure what kind of person Ahasverus is from his behavior in the folktales.

➢ You do more than just look at the character in relation to the plot; you look at all aspects of the character: both

- what is obvious

    and

- what is not so obvious.

You will analyze Ahasverus' character using a new graphic organizers called a character matrix.

This project will take a bit of concentration.

- You need to take your time to complete it.
- You should do the work a little at a time.

Implicit and Explicit in a Character

Two Key Points   An author tells about a character in two main ways: explicit traits and implicit or implied traits.

Explicit Statements   In the case of explicit traits or attributes or explicit characteristics, the author gives direct information and interpretive comments about the character, either the Wandering Jew or the shoemaker.

The narrator might:

- Describe the Wandering Jew's clothing, hair, eyes, etc.
- Tell about actions that the shoemaker does.
- Have the shoemaker directly say something that tells about himself.
- Give the thoughts that the Wandering Jew has.
- State what the Wandering Jew likes and dislikes, or how the he feels about another person or thing in the story.

The author directly explains these things. The reader doesn't really have to do anything except read.

Implicit Statements and Implied Judgment   Here the author doesn't directly state something about the Wandering Jew.

- The author tells you, the reader, in a description, example, thought, etc., about the Wandering Jew.
- Then you make a judgment about the Wandering Jew, based on the description, action, etc.

This is called implied judgment and allows a narrator to:

- Tell about an attitude or thought of the Wandering Jew without directly labeling it.
- Give an impression of the Wandering Jew. The reader has to interpret him from the impression.

Continued on next page

Implicit and Explicit in a Character, Continued

Example

Instead of saying a person is a glutton, the author describes how the boy gobbles up globs of food, using his hands and slobbering all over his mouth and chin. The author never says that the character is a glutton.

The author implies (never directly states) that the character is a glutton from the "piggy-like" description. You, the reader, come to the conclusion about the character's gluttony, by figuring out what the author means from his description. You get at the character from what the author implies, not directly states, about the character:

> **Again, this is called implied judgment. You, the reader, make a judgment about the character based on the author's implication or implicit statement. Nothing directly is said about the character of the person, in this case the boy.**

You will use implied judgment a lot in reading fiction.

Use a matrix to sketch Ahasverus's character

A Composite Sketch

Ahasverus is the name often given to the Wandering Jew/Shoemaker. We will this name from now on.

To give a complete sketch of Ahasverus you are going to create a composite character of the Wandering Jew/Shoemaker from three sources:

- The Shoemaker of Jerusalem (from Norway)
- "Song for the Wandering" Jew by William Wordsworth
- "The Wandering Jew" by James Whitcomb Riley

The matrix on the next page should help you pull various parts of the sketch from each of the resources above. Before you begin working on the matrix, read **Tips** on the next page.

Continued on next page

Use a matrix to sketch Ahasverus, Continued

Tips

Looking at **Composite Character Matrix: Ahasverus** on the next page, do the following:

For **Action/Behavior: What Ahasverus does:**

> ➢ Find an action or something that Ahasverus did in one of the poems.
>
> ➢ Write the example under **Examples.**
>
> ➢ Then write the poem from which you got the example under *From Where*.
>
> ➢ Continue on through all the selections looking for other examples of actions and list them in the same way.

When you have complete actions,

> ➢ Go on to **Physical Traits: How Ahasverus looks.**
> ➢ Find examples as you did for actions.
> ➢ Fill them in under **Examples**.
> ➢ Include the poem from which you got your example under *From Where*.

> **Note**: When filling in the poem under *From Where:*
>
> • Use **Riley** for examples from James Whitcomb Riley's "The Wandering Jew.
> • Use **Wordsworth** for an example from William Wordsworth's "Song for the Wandering Jew."
> • Use **Shoemaker** for examples from "The Shoemaker of Jerusalem" (from Norway).

> ➢ Continued with **Emotions: How Ahasverus feels**.
> ➢ Then finish up with **Expression: What he says and believes.**

We have filled in part of the matrix; you complete the rest of it.

Composite Character Matrix for Ahasverus

Trait/Attribute	Examples	From Where
Action/Behavior: What the Wandering Jew and the shoemaker each does	He ran away from Eli.	Shoemaker
Physical Traits: How each looks	"Terrible to look at: in rags, grimy face, … overgrown with white hair"	Shoemaker

Continued on next page

Composite Character Matrix, Continued

Trait/Attribute	Examples	*From Where*
Emotions: How the Wandering Jew and the shoemaker feel	The shoemaker was afraid to meet other people	Shoemaker
Expression: What each says and believes	Shoemaker feels his punishment	Shoemaker

Write your composite character sketch of Ahasverus from the Wandering Jew and the shoemaker

Tips

Now using your completed matrix, write a composite character sketch from "The Shoemaker of Jerusalem, "The Wandering Jew," and from "Song of the Wandering Jew."

➤ Write at least five paragraphs.

➤ Use the section titles under **Trait/Attribute** as the main part of the topic sentence for a paragraph.

➤ Get supporting sentences and details for each topic sentence from **Examples**.

➤ Make your last paragraph a summary of the character of the Wandering Jew.

The title of your writing should be: **"Composite Character Sketch: Ahasverus."**

Chapter XII
Weird and Wondrous

Introduction and Overview

Definition

Do you remember St. Perpetua's dragon or Martha's Tarasque? Well, dragons are not the only creatures that figure prominently in "r"eligious folktales. There are many other creatures that folks spun up, to account for "the unexplainable" relating to religion. In this chapter you will read about some of these creatures.

What to do:
Learning Objectives

➢ Compare and contrast two tales about the moon.

➢ Define exaggeration.

➢ Explain cause and effect in a strange dancing tale.

Companion Guide

This workbook is a companion to *"Snipp snapp snute, så er eventyret ute" – Folklore Reader and Critical Thinking Workbook*, which has additional critical thinking materials and reading selections.

Content

In this chapter you are going to read the following selections:

- Two selections about how the moon got its spots.

- A Russian "r"eligious folktale about a strange, little fellow.

- A story about a strange dance that possessed people during the Middle Ages.

A Sassy Man and a Toad

Who is he?   There are many "r"eligious stories about astronomical features like the sun and the moon. In the stories that follow, we look at how folks thought the moon got its spots. As you read each folktale, jot down the similarities and differences between these tales.

"The Man in the Moon"
Sabine Baring-Gould

When the moon is full, you can see dark spots on it. These are a man who went to live on the moon. Here is how it happened:

One Sunday, in the forest the man was wandering about. He had stolen a bunch of birch twigs and taken them on his back. Then a man, who was really the Lord, met him in the woods. He took the man to task because it was Sunday, saying: "I have to punish you. You can choose the punishment yourself. Would you like to be in the moon or the sun?"

The man answered: "If it must be, I would rather freeze on the moon than burn on the sun." And from that time on, he was the man in the moon.

> From: Baring-Gould, S. (Sabine). *Curious Myths of the Middle Ages*. London: Rivingtons, 1876. Not in copyright. At: http://en.wikipedia.org/wiki/Man_in_the_Moon and at http://www.archive.org/stream/curiousmythsofmi00bari/curiousmythsofmi00bari_djvu.txt

Another Version   Here is a "r"eligious folktale about the spots on the moon from a Native American tribe's ancient religion.

Continued on next page

A Sassy Man and a Toad, Continued

"Toad and the Moon"
Franz Boas

Spoxan was the moon, He invited the people to a feast. So many people went to the feast that his tent was soon crowded. Toad came along and found the house full. She asked where to sit. Spoxan answered, "There is no place to sit."

Toad was angry and returned to her own house. Then she made a heavy rain, which penetrated everything and put out lights and fires. As more people arrived, they crowded inside Spoxan's tent, saying, "Chief, where are we to sit? It is wet outside." At last, as the rain came pouring through the roof of the tent, all the people cried aloud, " Chief, where are we to sit? Where can we go to be out of the rain? "

They went from tent to tent, but it rained through them all. They went under canoes, but it rained through them too. Finally they saw a light from Toad's tent. When they arrived, they found Toad's tent very dry inside. They all went in, including Spoxan.

Then Toad jumped on Spoxan's face and sat there. At once the rain stopped. The people tried to pull Toad off Spoxan's face, but [they] did not succeed. The marks of Toad may still be seen on the moon.

From: Franz Boas et al. *Folk-tales of Salishan and Sahaptin tribes*. New York: American Folklore Society, 1917. Not in copyright. At: http://www.archive.org/details/folktalesofsalis00boas

Writing

- Did you keep track of the differences between the two folktales about how the moon got its spots?
- Write a couple of paragraphs about the differences between the two folktales.

A Giant and a Strange Russian Creature

Noah and the Giant

You know the Old Testament story about Noah and the flood. There are a number of "r"eligious folktales associated with Noah. Below is one. Pay attention to the exaggeration in this tale and the tale following it.

"Giant of The Flood"
Gertrude Landa

Just before the world was flooded all the animals gathered in front of the ark, and Noah carefully inspected them. As they began to enter the ark, Noah watched them closely. He seemed troubled. "I wonder," he said to himself, "how I shall obtain a unicorn, and how I shall get it into the ark."

"I can bring you a unicorn, Noah," a voice of thunder said to him, and turning round, Noah saw a giant named Og. "But you must agree to save me … from the flood.," Og added.

"Be gone [out of here]," cried Noah. "You are a demon, not a human being. I can have no dealings with you."

"Pity me," whined the giant. "See how my figure is shrinking. Once I was so tall that I could drink water from the clouds and toast fish on the sun. I am not afraid that I'll drown, but that the waters will destroy all the food … and I shall die ... of hunger."

Noah, however, only smiled. Then he grew serious again when Og brought a unicorn. It was as big as a mountain, although the giant said it was the smallest he could find. It lay down in front of the ark so gently and quiet that Noah saw … he must save it. For some time, he was puzzled what to do, but at last he had a bright idea: He attached the huge beast to the ark by a rope fastened to its horn so that it could swim alongside and be fed.

Og seated himself on a mountain near by and watched the rain pouring down. Faster and faster, it fell in torrents until the rivers overflowed, and the waters began to rise rapidly … and to sweep all things away. Noah stood gloomily before the door of the ark until the water reached his neck. Then it swept him inside. The door closed with a bang, and the ark rose … on the flood and began to move along. The unicorn swam alongside, and as it passed Og, the giant jumped on to its back.

Continued on next page

A Giant and a Strange Russian Creature, Continued

"See, Noah," Og cried, with a huge chuckle, "you will have to save me after all. I will snatch all the food you put through the window for the unicorn."

Noah saw that it was useless to argue with Og, who might, indeed, sink the ark with his tremendous strength. "I will make a bargain with you, Og" he shouted from a window. "I will feed you, but you must promise to be a servant to my descendants." Og was very hungry, so he accepted the conditions and devoured his first breakfast.

The rain continued to fall in great sheets that shut out the light of day. Inside the ark, however, all was bright and cheerful, for Noah had collected the most precious stones of the earth and had used them for the windows. Their radiance lighted up three stories in the ark. Some animals were troublesome, and Noah got no sleep at all.

In one corner, a bird slept the whole time. This was the phoenix.

"Wake up," said Noah, one day. "It is feeding time."

"Thank you," answered the bird. "I saw you were very busy, Noah, so I didn't want to trouble you."

"You are a good bird," said Noah, much touched, "therefore you shall never die."

One day the rain ceased [stopped], the clouds rolled away, and the sun shone brilliantly again. How strange the world looked! It was like a vast ocean. Only water could be seen everywhere, and just one or two of the highest mountain tops peeped above the flood. All the world had been drowned. Noah gazed on the desolate [empty] scene from one of the windows, with tears in his eyes.

Og, riding gaily on the unicorn behind the ark, was quite happy. "Ha, ha!" he laughed gleefully. "I shall be able to eat and drink as much as I like now and shall never be troubled by those tiny little creatures, the mortals [human beings]."

"Don't be so sure," said Noah. "Those tiny mortals shall be your masters and shall outlive you and the whole race of giants and demons."

The giant did not relish [enjoy] this prospect. He knew that whatever Noah prophesied would come true, and he was so sad that he ate no food for two days and began to grow smaller and thinner. He became more and more unhappy as day by day the water subsided and the mountains began to appear. At last, the ark rested on Mount Ararat, and Og's long ride came to an end.

"I will soon leave you, Noah," he said. "I shall wander round the world to see what is left of it."

"You can't go until I allow you to," said Noah. "Have you forgotten our agreement so soon? You must be my servant. I have work for you to do."

Continued on next page

A Giant and a Strange Russian Creature, Continued

Giants are not fond of work, and Og, who was the father of all the giants, was particularly lazy. He wanted only to eat and sleep, but he knew he was in Noah's power, and he shed bitter tears when he saw the land appear again. "Stop crying," commanded Noah. "Do you wish to flood the world once more, with your big tears?"

So, Og sat on a mountain and rocked from side to side, weeping silently to himself. He watched the animals leave the ark. Then he had to do all the hard work when Noah's children built their houses. Daily, he complained that he was shrinking to the size of the mortals, for Noah said there was not too much food. One day Noah said to him, "Come with me, Og. I am going around the world. I am commanded to plant fruit and flowers to make the earth beautiful. I need your help."

For many days, Noah and Og wandered all over the earth. Og was compelled [forced] to carry the heavy bag of seeds. The last thing Noah planted was the grape vine. "What food or drink is this?" asked Og.

"Both food and drink," replied Noah. "It can be eaten, or its juice made into wine." As he planted it, he blessed the grape. "Be thou," he said, "a plant pleasing to the eye, bear fruit that will be food for the hungry and a health-giving drink to the thirsty and sick."

Og only grunted. "I will offer up a sacrifice to this wonderful fruit," he said. "May I do so now that our labors [heavy work] are over?"

Noah agreed, and the giant brought a sheep, a lion, a pig and a monkey. First, he slaughtered the sheep, then the lion. "When a man tastes a few drops of wine," Og said, "he shall be as harmless as a sheep. When he takes a little more he shall be as strong as a lion."

Then Og began to dance around the plant, and he killed the pig and the monkey. Noah was very much surprised. "I am giving your descendants two extra blessings," said Og, chuckling. He rolled over and over on the ground in great glee and then said: "When a man drinks too much of the juice of the grapevine, then he shall become a beast like the pig. If he still continues to drink, he shall behave foolishly like a monkey."

And that is why … too much wine makes a man silly.

From: Gertrude Landa. *Jewish fairy tales and legends*. New York: Bloch Publishing Co, 1919. Not in copyright.

Continued on next page

A Giant and a Strange Russian Creature, Continued

"Potanka"
Aleksandr Nikolaevich Afanasev

Granny was preparing to bake the holy bread, but she forgot to bless it. Potanka came and sat right in the dough. Suddenly, granny remembered that she hadn't said the blessing over the dough. She came right back and made the sign of the Cross over the bread. Potanka leaped up, but too late. Granny had already picked up the dough and tossed it out, and Potanka with it!

On the road, all the pigs battered the bread about from place to place, naturally with Potanka in it. He just couldn't get away for three days. Finally, he found a little slit in the bread and got out. He ran away without looking back.

He met some comrades. They asked him, "Where have you been, Potanka?"

"May old granny be cursed," he replied.

> **"She was kneading the dough and had not said the blessing; so I ran up and squatted in it. She grabbed hold of me and made the Cross. For three whole days, I couldn't get away: the pigs poked me about and me with no way to escape ! Never, never again will I sit in granny's dough."**

From: Aleksandr Nikolaevich Afanasev. *Narodnyia russkiia skazki i legendy*. Berlin: Izdatel'stvo I.P. Ladyzhnikova. Not in copyright. (Translated by David Garnett)

Writing   Now that you have read these two "r"eligious folktales about weird creatures, write about how each take uses exaggeration. Write about each tale in separate paragraph.

Some Strange Dancing

"Frau Marta's Dance"

It was July 15, 1518. Frau Marta Shuhmacher stepped out onto the little cobblestone street outside her front door. Today would be hot and humid in Strasbourg [a town in France]. She wondered if her husband would sell enough sandals to feed the mouths of their children. The last years had been nothing but trouble; she had had to scrape to just exist. No one wanted to buy shoes; sometimes her husband couldn't get any materials to work with. Marta just wanted to stare into space, not pay attention to anything – to be away from it all.

Suddenly Marta felt her legs move as though she was about to start a dancing step. She looked down at her feet for a moment. That was the last time she did. Her legs were moving on their own. A rhythm took her whole body. She started to whirl in dizzy movement. The whole world blurred and ran around her in one continuous movement. Then her mind went blank; she was as though hypnotized. Her feet kept dancing. Her body moved out onto the street. Occasionally, she lurched forward in a little jump or hop. Sometimes, she moved on tiptoe, scraping her cloth shoes on the rough stones.

"Papa," yelled little Franz, "Mama is dancing on the street like the others. Come see!"

Herr Peter Shuhmacher came up beside his son and peered out into the dusty morning air. "Marta," he said. "Stop this nonsense and get back in the house – right away!" His face crimped in worry and vexation. "Here we go again. When I tell her do something, I get this kind of thing!" he murmured to himself. "Get back here," he repeated angrily.

All was to no avail. Marta kept on whirling and stamping, just like the other dancers who had danced uncontrollably the week before: She was jumping, stomping, pirouetting, leaping, and twirling. Those other dancers had behaved like carnival dancers out of control. And they didn't stop to rest, to eat, or to drink. The only way to stop such a frenzy was total fatigue, so heavy and exhausting that a dancer just dropped onto the ground and slept. But then as soon as they awoke, the contorted dance returned. Was this to be Marta's fate too?

By now, a group of housewives from the neighborhood, together with various and sundry beggars, tradesmen, and school children, were pointing and laughing at Frau Shuhmacher. Some gypsies were stepping up to Marta, almost in her face, copying the strange grimace and facial ticks she had started to make. Peter Shuhmacher rushed up, shoving them aside and tried to push his wife back to their front door.

There was no stopping his wife. She was hopping in a mad dance. She started out down the road. It was like some kind of disorganized holiday parade. Occasionally, she stumbled and fell, but instead of getting up she lay on the hard ground as though in a daze. A couple of peddlers helped her up. As soon as she was on her feet, they took off again. "She just doesn't seem to know what is happening, what she is doing?" whispered a watchman to his friend. "I am reporting this to the mayor – it's too strange."

Continued on next page

264

Some Strange Dancing, Continued

The mayor was already aware something was happening. He had first thought it was another one of those hunger protests that had become more common with the failing harvests in recent years. When the watchman explained the strange occurrence, the mayor decided that the local bishop should know about these weird circumstances. He sent the watchman to request that the bishop meet him in the town square.

By the time the mayor with the town council and the bishop with his priests had gathered by the town fountain, Marta was dancing in bare feet. Her cloth shoes had been ripped to bits by the uneven stones on the street. Her feet were bleeding. She had scraped herself on her arms and legs from the many falls. Her clothes were all messed up, covered with dirt and mud. Her little white wife-cap had fallen from her head, and her hair was wet and matted with sweat and dust. Nothing stopped her though. She paid attention to no one. Her feet just carried her on, jumping, twirling, tapping and thumping. A couple of housewives were walking near her, one with a little food; the other with a jug of water. They had understood that these energetic, frenzied antics would tire Marta out.

"She is possessed by a demon." proclaimed the bishop without hesitation. "We must carry her to the chapel of St. Vitus. He will cure her of this fit."

"Agreed," said the mayor. "I will tell her husband. We can take her this evening."

****

The ride to St. Vitus Chapel was anything but uneventful as Marta's body kept on with its agitated movements: Once she stood up in the wagon and tried to prance about. Later, she tried to jump out and to dance along the road beside the cart. When she was finally forced to sit down, she jiggled constantly: hands, head, hips, legs and feet – all moved to some kind of soundless beat. And her eyes just stared ahead, not blinking. Not a sound, only occasional grunts from her labored gasps.

When they arrived at the chapel of St. Vitus, Herr Peter and the men with him had to drag Marta into the little building. Her feet seem to want to dance off into the surrounding forest. They had to lift her with her feet dancing on air. It took four strong men to control her and carry her under her arms.

When they were all inside, it seemed as if Frau Shuhmacher was just going to keep on dancing in her trance.

"Hold her," commanded the bishop. "Here, put these red slippers on her feet. I am sure they will help her."

"Why?" asked Herr Peter. "I don't understand."

"Look at the icon of St. Vitus – the colors," said one of the priests. Peter and the other men took a careful look at St. Vitus. He was painted wearing a red cap, red boots, and his robe had a red border.

"It is a way of gaining the saint's favor," continued the bishop.

Continued on next page

Some Strange Dancing, Continued

After much fussing (you can imagine how difficult it was to put slippers on those jiggling feet.), the men finally got the slippers on Frau Shuhmacher's feet. As the men carried her toward the little crucifix, her head bobbed about. Slowly, her eyes fluttered shut; finally her head sank onto her chest. Her feet slowly stopped their frantic movements. Marta's whole body went limp and heavy. They put her down gently before the altar. Gasping from the exertion of carrying the woman, the men just stood quietly, looking at the motionless figure in front of the altar. They all waited.

Then Frau Marta Shuhmacher gradually opened her eyes. For the first time since she had started her driven movements, she moved her mouth. A little smile of recognition spread over her face. She nodded her head at her husband. Although totally worn-out from her ordeal, Marta was serene and peaceful again. Her frantic "dance" had stopped.

This story developed by David Garnett is based on John Waller's *The Dancing Plague*. Source book, Inc. ISBN 978-1-40221-943-6.

Mini-exercise   Complete the study tables; follow the directions in each table.

What precipitated [caused] Frau Marta's falling, jumping, kicking, etc.?   (Circle **only one letter**.)

a.	The reoccurrence of a childhood illness.
b.	An allergy to the shoes that her husband made.
c.	A strange dancing that seemed to come from nowhere.
d.	A bad dancing teacher who didn't really know how to teach.

How did people react to Frau Marta's weird "dance"?

(Circle **all the letters** that apply.)

a.	Some people were angry.
b.	Other people paid no attention.
c.	Others tried to help Frau Shuhmacher.
d.	Lots of people got on their knees and prayed for her.

Find cause and effect in "Frau Marta's Strange Dance"

What to do You are going to look at the cause and its effects in the story. The cause had many different effects on:

- Frau Marta
- Her family
- Neighbors and townspeople
- The authorities in the town

You are going to sort out the various effects on the different folks in the story by using **Cause and Effect for Frau Marta's Dance** on the next page.

Read Tips below before filling in the table.

Tips

- ➢ In the column labeled **Who was affected** we have put in various people from the story. All were in some way affected by what happened to Frau Shuhmacher.

- ➢ After each person or group of people you need to write in the effects that Frau Marta's behavior had on the person/people.

- ➢ We have filled in a couple for you.

- ➢ We have left the final section of the table blank so that you can fill in any additional cause and effect(s) from the story which you think we have missed.

Cause and Effect for Frau Marta's Dance

Cause	Who was affected	How affected
Weird Dance	Frau Marta	1.
		2.
		3.
		4.
		5.
		6.
		7.
		8.
		9. Her feet got bloodied.
	Herr Shuhmacher	1.
		2.
		3.
	Neighborhood Women	1.
		2.
		3.
		4.

Continued on next page

Cause and Effect for Frau Marta's Dance, Continued

Cause	Who was affected	How affected	
Weird Dance	*The Authorities: Mayor, Priests, etc.*	1.	
		2.	
		3.	
		4.	
	Other People in the Neighborhood	1.	
		2.	
		Gypsies made fun of her.	
		1.	
		2.	
		3.	
		4.	

Writing   Using your completed cause and effect table, write about the effects of Frau Marta's strange dance on the various other people in the story.

For Notes

Chapter XIII
Where religions meet

Introduction and Overview

Definition

This stanza from a hymn called "The Word of God" introduces the topic of this chapter.

> **"From Sinai's cliff it echoed,**
> **It breathed from Buddha's tree,**
> **It charmed in Athens' market,**
> **The hammer stroke of Luther,**
> **The Pilgrims' seaside prayer,**
> **The oracles of Concord**
> **One holy word declare."**

> From: William Channing Gannett's (1840-1923) hymn "The Word of God." in *Singing the Living Tradition*.

Do you have an idea about the selections of "r"eligious folklore in this chapter? Keep this stanza in mind as you read the different selections.

What to do: Learning Objectives

In this chapter you are going to:

➤ Define the relationship between characters in a story with the help of a relationship organizer.

➤ Compare and contrast two stories about religious conversions.

Companion Guide

This workbook is a companion to *"Snipp snapp snute, så er eventyret ute" – Folklore Reader and Critical Thinking Workbook*, which has additional critical thinking materials and reading selections.

Continued on next page

Introduction and Overview, Continued

Chapter Components

A text or group of texts that you will read. Most of the writing and other work you do require you to read and refer to these text resource(s).

Any of a number of activities or exercises which you need to complete. These activities may include:

- Vocabulary exercises.
- Questions to answer.
- Study tables to complete
- Thinking organizers (graphic or picture diagrams) to fill out.
- Written work to plan, organize, and write.

All these activities should help you to read and understand the texts or to write about them. You may have to complete a project, which requires limited research.

Content: Selections

- "Simon, the Righteous" by Austine Park and Ina Lipsomb.

- "The Aged Planter and Hadrian" by Herman Hurwitz.

- "The Choice" by Rose G. Lurie.

- Vladimir's Conversion from *The Russian Primary Chronicle*.

- St. Francis meets Sultan Malik al-Kamil.

Alexander the Great and the Hebrews

Background   Alexander the Great was the most famous Greek leader in the ancient world. He came from Macedonia, which is in northern Greece. At the height of his power, his empire included most of the Middle East, Iran, and parts of India. Read below about how he interacted with the Hebrews in Syria.

"Simon, The Righteous"
Austine Park and Ina Lipsomb

Simon was … the high priest among the Jews during [the time] of Alexander the Great, about the year 3000 BCE. The Jews found no cause to oppose this … [Alexander]. … When he came to Syria on his way to Egypt, the Jews joined with the other peoples … [to honor Alexander].

… As the representative of [the Hebrews], Simon traveled to greet the conqueror. He was dressed in his priestly robes and was attended by a number of priests and nobles. Alexander at once approached the high priest and greeted him warmly. When his officers expressed their astonishment at this mark of … [reverence], Alexander told them that this Simon, clad in the same robes he now wore, had appeared in a dream and promised him [Alexander] success in the war.

Alexander was shown around the temple by Simon. On entering, Alexander, who was a pagan, said, "Blessed be the Lord of this house." The warrior was charmed with the beauty of the temple and expressed a desire to have a statue of himself erected as a remembrance between the porch and the altar. Simon informed him that it was forbidden to erect any statue or image of a person in the temple or on its walls. Simon then promised that, as a remembrance of Alexander's visit, male children born to Jews that year should all be named Alexander, which was not a traditional Hebrew name. That is the way all Alexander's obtained their names.

Alexander continued to be … pleased with and friendly toward Simon. He granted the Jews religious freedom and released them from all tributes and taxes during the Sabbath year. He also allowed Jews to enter his army and assist in his conquests.

Adapted from: Austine Park and Ina Lipsomb. *The Sacred Books and Early Literature of The East with Historical Surveys of the Chief Writings of Each Nation*, 1917. Not in copyright. At: http://www.archive.org/stream/sacredbooksearly03hornuoft/sacredbook searly03hornuoft_djvu.txt

---

Continued on next page

Alexander the Great and the Hebrews, Continued

Mini-exercise   Complete the study tables. Follow the directions in each table.

Alexander the Great was positive toward Simon because _____

(Circle **all the letters** that apply.)

a.	Simon promised to make the Hebrews worship the conqueror.
b.	Alexander realized how important a person Simon was.
c.	Alexander wanted to make fools of his own followers.
d.	Simon promised Alexander victories in a dream.

Alexander showed his appreciation for Simon by _____

(Circle **all the letters** that apply.)

a.	Making Simon his deputy and assistant.
b.	Granting the Hebrews religious freedom.
c.	Donating a lot of gold to the Hebrew temple.
d.	Allowing the Hebrews to serve in his army.

Writing   Write a short paragraph on the difference between Alexander and his followers:

- How each looked at Simon.

- Use actions and words of Alexander and his courtiers to support the difference.

Emperor Hadrian and a Hebrew Farmer

Background   Hadrian was emperor of the ancient Roman empire from 117 CE to 138 CE. His rule was peaceful, with few conflicts. He was very interested in the arts: Tivoli gardens in Roman and numerous other buildings and monuments were built during his reign. Abroad, the famous Hadrian's Wall to separate the civilized world of the Romans from the warring barbarians of Scotland was built in Britain. Read about how he treated an old Hebrew farmer.

"The Aged Planter and Hadrian"
Hyman Hurwitz

"Thou shalt rise up before the hoary head, and honor the
face of the old man, and fear thy God. I am the Lord."
Levit. xix. 32.

Emperor Hadrian, passing near the town of Tiberias in Galilee, saw an old Hebrew digging a large trench in order to plant some fig trees. "If you had properly worked in your youth," said Hadrian, "you would not need to work so hard in your later years."

"I have worked well in my early days, nor will I neglect the evening of my life; and let God do what he thinks best," replied the man.

"How old are you, good man?" asked the emperor.

"A hundred years," was the reply.

"What," exclaimed Emperor Hadrian, impressed, "a hundred years old, and you are still planting trees! Can you ever hope to enjoy the fruits of thy labor?"

"Great Emperor," replied the hoary-headed man, "yes, I hope if God permits, that I may eat the fruit of these very trees; if not, my children will. Haven't my forefathers planted trees for me? … Shall I not do the same for my children?"

Hadrian, pleased with the honest man's reply, said, "Well, old man, if you should live to see the fruit of these trees, let me know. Do you hear me, old fella? "With these words, Hadrian left him.

Continued on next page

Emperor Hadrian and a Hebrew Farmer, Continued

The old man did live long enough to see the fruits of his industry. The trees flourished and bore excellent fruit. As soon as they were ripe, the old man gathered the choicest figs, put them in a basket, and marched off to the emperor's residence. Hadrian happened to look out one of the palace windows. Seeing a man, bent with age, with a basket on his shoulders, standing near the gate, he ordered the old man to be admitted to the palace. "What do you want, old man?" demanded Emperor Hadrian.

"May it please your majesty," replied the man, "Do you remember seeing once a very old man planting some fig trees? Then you desired him, if ever he should gather the fruit from those trees, to let you know. I am that old man, and this is the fruit of those very trees. May it please you graciously to accept them as gratitude for your majesty's stopping and speaking with me."

Pleased to see a person so long-lived, with full use of all his faculties and so honest, the emperor asked the old man to be seated. Ordering the basket to be emptied of the fruit, the emperor filled it with gold and gave it to the old man, as a present. Some courtiers who witnessed this unusual scene, exclaimed, "Is it possible that our great emperor should show so much honor to a miserable Hebrew!"

"Why shouldn't I honor him whom God has honored?" replied Hadrian. "Look at his age and follow his example." The emperor then very graciously dismissed the old man, who went home highly pleased and delighted.

****

The old man came home and showed the gold he had received. The people were all astonished. Among the neighbors, there was a silly, covetous [greedy] woman, who, seeing so much treasure for a few figs, imagined that the emperor must be very fond of that fruit; she therefore hastily ran home and told her husband, "You, son of a wretch, what are you waiting for? Didn't you hear that Caesar Hadrian is very fond of figs? Go, take some to him, and you will be as rich as your neighbor."

The foolish husband, unable to stand his wife's complaints, took a large sack, filled it with figs, put it on his shoulders, and after much bother, finally arrived at the palace gate. He immediately demanded to see the emperor. When asked what he wanted, he answered, that he had heard that the emperor was very fond of figs. He said that he had brought a whole sack full, for which he expected a great reward.

The officer on duty reported all this to the emperor. Hadrian could not help smiling at the man's foolishness and impertinence [arrogance], so he said to the officer: "Yes, let the fool have his reward. Let him remain where he is, and let every one who enters the gate take one of the figs, and throw it at his face, until all the figs are gone; then let him depart." The order was punctually [on the spot] executed [carried out]... .

Continued on next page

Emperor Hadrian and a Hebrew Farmer, Continued

The wretched neighbor, abused, pelted, and derided [insulted], instead of wishing for gold, wished only to see the bottom of his bag. After much patience, and still more pain, he had his wish. The bag being empty, the poor fellow was dismissed. Dejected and sorrowful, he hastened home.

Meanwhile, his wife was all the while considering how to dispose of the expected treasure, calculating how many fine caps, gowns, and cloaks she would purchase. She imagined how fine she should look and how her neighbors would stare at her so finely dressed. She waited most impatiently for her husband's return.

At last, he arrived, and though she saw the bag empty, she imagined that his pockets at least were full of gold. Without greeting him and hardly allowing him to catch his breath, she hastily asked him what good luck he had had. Her wretched husband replied:

> **"Have patience, wretched woman, … have patience, and I will tell you. I have had both great and good luck. My great luck was that I took figs, not peaches, to the emperor; otherwise, I should have been stoned to death with their pits. My good luck was that the figs were ripe. If they had been unripe, I would have all my brains bashed out of my head because figs are so hard when they are not ripe."**

Adapted from: Hyman Hurwitz. *Hebrew tales: selected and translated from the writings of the ancient Hebrew sages*. Revised and edited by George Alexander Kohut. New York: Bloch Publishing Co., 1911. Not in copy right. At: http://www.archive.org/stream/hebrewtalesselec00hurwiala/hebrewtalesselec00hurwiala_djvu.txt

---

Mini-exercise   Complete the study tables that follow. Read the directions in each table.

Continued on next page

Emperor Hadrian and a Hebrew Farmer, Continued

Look the quotation below:

You shall rise up before the hoary [old, worn] head, and honor the face of the old man, and fear thy God. I am the Lord.

Leviticus. xix. 32.

Now, write your answers to the following questions:
- **Which character in the tale is the quotation about?**
- **To what person in the story might this quotation be spoken?**
- **How does this person fulfill this quotation?**

(Write your answers below.)

Continued on next page

Emperor Hadrian and a Hebrew Farmer, Continued

How would you say the first farmer regarded Emperor Hadrian?

(Circle **all the letters** that apply.)

a.	He treated the emperor with respect.
b.	He was aggressive toward Emperor Hadrian.
c.	He was honest in what he said to Emperor Hadrian.
d.	He played the fool with the emperor.

How did the second farmer's wife treat her husband?

(Circle **all the letters** that apply.)

a.	The wife thought her husband was wise and respected him highly.
b.	She considered him lazy and felt she had to force him to do things.
c.	She thought he was a hard-working man, but a bit slow.
d.	The wife thought her husband was a good-for-nothing wretch.

Which of the two farmers did Emperor Hadrian respect?

(Circle **all the letters** that apply.)

a.	He respected the first farmer because he was trying to get rich.
b.	He respected the second farmer because he was very aggressive.
c.	He respected the second farmer because he was a real go-getter.
d.	He respected the first farmer because he was honest and truthful.

Look at Hadrian's relationship to each farmer

What to do

You are going to define the:

> ➢ Relationship between Emperor Hadrian and the first farmer.
> ➢ Relationship between the emperor and the second farmer.
> ➢ Character of the emperor from his relationship to the two men.

Basically, figure out why the emperor behaved the way he did to each farmer. This should give you a good idea of the emperor's character and the kind of people he liked and disliked.

Continued on next page

Look at Hadrian's relationship to each farmer, Continued

Tips
To help you decide the kind of person the emperor liked fill out the table below:

➢ Go back to the story and read carefully about each farmer.
➢ Write in the table what farmer I (the first farmer) did or how he behaved, each in separate box.
➢ Then looking at the emperor, check how he reacted to farmer I's behavior, i. e. positively or negatively.

Follow the same steps for farmer II (the second farmer).

Relationship Table for Hadrian and the Two Farmers

What farmer I did (behaved)	How Hadrian reacted			What farmer II did (behaved)	How Hadrian reacted	
	Positive	Negative			Positive	Negative
Believed in himself	X					
Thought of his grandchildren				Thought only about money		X

Continued on next page

Look at Hadrian's relationship to each farmer, Continued

Writing   Using your completed relationship table and the story, write at least two paragraphs:

- The first is about the kinds of people that Emperor Hadrian probably liked.

- The second, about people whom he probably disliked.

Be sure to give examples from your table and from the story.

Two Stories about Conversion

Where religions meet   Do you remember Olaf Tryggvason, who converted Norway to Christianity? He had to use force and violence to enforce Christianity. Clearly, two religions meet in any situation where one religion is trying to convert people. You are going to read two stories about conversions.

- One story is about how a pagan warrior tribe in their empire near Russia, the Khazars, was converted around 700 CE.
- The second story is about how early Russia was converted.

Khazar Conversion

24. The Choice
Rose G. Lurie

Once there was an empire called Khazaria, located near present-day Russia. It was ruled by a people, called Khazars (Kazars). [The Khazars were a Turkic-speaking tribe. Many years earlier they had come from the Far East near Siberia.] They were very warlike. So their khans (kings) went from country to country fighting with people. All ... nations feared them.

These rough people hardly had any religion at all, but on their travels they met Christians, Moslems, and Jews. When Bulent, one of their kings, met these people and learned about their religions, he became greatly dissatisfied with his own. Day after day, Bulent thought about his people's religion. One time when he was greatly worried, he had ...a dream. It seemed to him that an angel came to him and said:

Continued on next page

Two Stories about Conversion, Continued

Khazar Conversion, Continued

> **"You do not serve God in the right**
> **way. Send for a Jew, a Christian and**
> **a Moslem. Let them each explain his**
> **religion to you. Then you will choose**
> **the best for your own [people]."**

The angel disappeared, and Bulent awoke, He ordered one of his wise men to come to him at once. The wise man was tired and sleepy. Why should he be taken out of his bed at night? But the king's orders must be obeyed. Therefore he dressed quickly and came before Bulent. Then Bulent spoke to him and said: "Tell me, Wise One, Tell me true, What does your God mean to you?"

… The wise man answered:

> **"God is a Spirit,**
> **Far removed is He,**
> **How can He care**
> **For you or for me?"**

Bulent was not satisfied with this explanation. "Bah," he said. "No--no. A god who does not guard over my kingdom, a god who does not care about me, can't be my god."

A few days later, Bulent ordered that a Christian monk should come to him. When the monk entered in his long black robe and three-cornered hat … , Bulent was interested. Again he said:

> **"Tell me monk,**
> **Tell me true: What religion pleases you?**

The monk answered:

> **"My religion**
> **As you see,**
> **My religion**
> **Pleases me."**

Continued on next page

Khazar Conversion, Continued

Bulent asked: "If you had to choose between the religion of the Jew and that of the Moslem, which would you choose?"

The monk answered, "I would choose the Jewish religion. It is the oldest, and our religion is based on it."

Bulent thanked the monk for his advice. The next day Bulent said: "I shall call a Moslem and find out what he has to say." So … a Moslem came before Bulent. He had a very dark skin, darker than any skin that Bulent had ever seen. His long grey gown and the turban around his head made him very attractive. Bulent asked him the same question that he had asked … the others: "Tell me Moslem, tell me true: Which religion pleases you?"

The Moslem answered:

> **"My religion**
> **As you see,**
> **My religion**
> **Pleases me."**

"If you had to choose between the religion of the Jew, and that of the monk, which would you choose?"

The Moslem answered: "I would choose the Jewish religion. It is the oldest, and our religion is based on it." Bulent thanked him for his advice. The next day he called a Jew and put his question: "Tell me Jew, tell me true: Which religion pleases you?"

The Jew answered:

> **"My religion**
> **As you see,**
> **My religion**
> **Pleases me."**

Bulent asked:

> **"Tell me, Jew,**
> **Tell me true,**
> **What does God**
> **Mean to you?"**

Continued on next page

Two Stories about Conversion, Continued

Khazar Conversion, Continued

The Jew answered:

> **"Love thy neighbor as thyself**
> **And know the prophets too.**
> **This, the message of the Jew**
> **Forever will be true."**

Bulent then turned to the Jew and said:

> **"You will be happy to know that I**
> **asked the monk this question: 'If you**
> **had to choose between the religion of**
> **the Jew and that of the Moslem,**
> **which would you choose?' He**
> **answered: 'The Jewish religion.' "I**
> **then asked the Moslem a similar**
> **question. He answered: 'The Jewish**
> **religion.'**
>
> **"Now, all religions seem good to me if**
> **they teach us that there is one God**
> **who is the Father of us all, and that**
> **all men are brothers. But as the**
> **Jewish religion is the oldest, my folk**
> **and I shall come to you." ...**

So Bulent and his Khazar people converted to Judaism. ...

Adapted from: Rose G. Lurie. *The Great March*. (Not in copyright). At:
http://www.sacred-texts.com/jud/tgm/tgm37.htm

Continued on next

Look at the conversion of Bulent and the Khazars

Mini-exercise   Complete the study tables below. Follow the directions in each table.

The monk and the Moslem both recommended_____

(Circle **only the letter** that applies.)

a.	Christianity because it preached mercy.
b.	Judaism because it espoused humility.
c.	Islam because you had to prostrate yourself before Allah.
d.	Judaism because it was the basis for the two other religions.

Two beliefs Bulent found common to Islam, Christianity, and Judaism were _____

(Circle **only the letter** that applies.)

a.	The pope was recognized by all three religions and was considered the supreme leader.
b.	All three believed in the trinity and had a credo about God.
c.	All men are brothers, and there is one God over all of us.
d.	Jesus is the prophet of all three religions and was a just leader.

Two Stories about Conversion, Continued

Background

Prince Vladimir … [ruled Russia] from 980 to 1015 CE. He wanted to choose a religion for Russia. He looked at several:

- Islam, which had been carried to central Asia by Arab armies.
- Judaism, which the Khazars on the Lower Volga had adopted.
- Western Christianity [and known as Roman Catholicism], professed by the Germans.
- Christianity of the East, from Byzantium and called Orthodoxy.

As you read about what religion Vladimir selected and how he made his choice, think about the similarities to and differences from the conversion of Bulent, the Khazar khan.

Vladimir's Conversion

Vladimir Christianizes Russia
From The Russian Primary Chronicle

[In 987 CE] Vladimir summoned together his boyars [nobles] and the city elders, [saying to] … to them:

> "Behold, the Bulgars, [who are Muslims,] came before me urging me to accept their religion. Then came the Germans and praised their own faith [which is called Roman Catholicism]. … After them came the Jews. Finally the Greeks appeared, criticizing all other faiths but commending their own, and they spoke at length, telling the history of the whole world from its beginning. Their words were artful, and it was wondrous to listen and pleasant to hear them. They preach the existence of another world. 'Whoever adopts our religion and then dies shall arise and live forever. But whosoever embraces another faith shall be consumed with fire in the next world.' What is your opinion on this subject, and what do you answer?"

Continued on next page

Two Stories about Conversion, Continued

Vladimir's Conversion, Continued

The boyars and the elders replied: "You know, O prince, that no man condemns his own possessions, but praises them instead. If you desire to make certain, you have servants at your disposal. Send them to inquire about the ritual of each and how he worships God."

Their counsel [advice] pleased the prince so that he chose good and wise men to the number of ten, and directed them to go first among the Bulgars and inspect their faith. The emissaries went their way, and when they arrived at their destination they beheld the strange actions of the Bulgars and their worship in the mosque; then they returned to their own country.

Vladimir then instructed them to go… among the Germans, and examine their faith, and finally to visit the Greeks. They thus went into Germany, and after viewing the German ceremonial, they proceeded to Constantinople where they appeared before the Emperors of Byzantium. The emperors asked on what mission they had come. They reported to the emperors Basil and Constantine [why they were visiting Constantinople]. When the emperors heard their words, they rejoiced and did them great honor on that very day.

[The next day], the emperors sent a message to the patriarch [the religious leader of the Orthodox Church] to inform him that a Russian delegation had arrived to examine the Greek faith, and directed him to prepare the church and the clergy, and to array himself in his sacerdotal [religious] robes, so that the Russians might behold the glory of the God of the Greeks. When the patriarch received these commands, he [ordered] the clergy to assemble, and they performed the customary rites. They burned incense, and the choirs sang hymns.

The emperors accompanied the Russians to the church and [showed them the church], calling their attention to the beauty of the edifice, the chanting, and the offices of the archpriest [chief priest] and the ministry of the deacons, while they explained to Vladimir's emissaries the worship of the [orthodox] God. The Russians were astonished, and in their wonder praised the Greek rites. Then the emperors said: "Go … to your native country," and … dismissed them with valuable presents and great honor.

Think about: Which rite do you think the emissaries will favor? Why?

Continued on next page

Two Stories about Conversion, Continued

Vladimir's Conversion, Continued

The [Russian delegation] returned to Russia, and Prince Vladimir called together his boyars and the elders. Vladimir then … commanded the [envoys] to speak out before his vassals. The envoys reported:

> **"When we journeyed among the Bulgars, we beheld how they worship in their temple, called a mosque, while they stand ungirt. The Bulgarian bows, sits down, looks hither and thither like one possessed, and there is no happiness among them, but instead only sorrow and a dreadful stench. Their religion is not good.**
>
> **"Then we went among the Germans and saw them performing many ceremonies in their temples; but we beheld no glory there.**
>
> **"Then we went on to Greece, and the Greeks led us to the edifices [magnificent buildings] where they worship their God, and we knew not whether we were in heaven or on earth. For on earth there is no such splendor or such beauty -- we are at a loss how to describe it. We know only that God dwells there among men. … Their service is fairer than the ceremonies of other nations. We cannot forget that beauty! 'Every man, after tasting something sweet, is afterward unwilling to accept that which is bitter'; therefore we [could not stay] longer there."**

Then the boyars spoke and said: "O, Prince Vladimir, if the Greek faith were evil, it would not have been adopted by your grandmother Olga, who was wiser than all other men." Vladimir then inquired where they should all accept baptism, and they replied that the decision rested with him.

Continued on next page

Two Stories about Conversion, Continued

Vladimir's Conversion, Continued

After a year had passed, in 6496 (988CE), Prince Vladimir marched with an armed force against Kherson, a Greek Byzantine city [located in present-day Ukraine]. The people of Kherson barricaded themselves [inside their city]. Vladimir halted at the farther side of the city beside the bay, a bowshot from the town. ... .

... Vladimir besieged the town. Eventually ... the inhabitants of Kherson became exhausted, and Vladimir warned them that if they did not surrender, he would remain on the spot for three years. When they failed to heed this threat, Vladimir marshaled [gathered together] his troops and ordered the construction of an earthwork in the direction of the city. While this work was under construction, the inhabitants dug a tunnel under the city wall, stole the heaped-up earth, and carried it into the city, where they piled it up in the center of the town. But the soldiers kept on building, and Vladimir persisted.

Then a man of Kherson, Anastasius, shot, into the Russian [Vladimir's] camp, an arrow on which he had written: "There are springs behind you to the east, from which water flows in pipes. Dig down and cut them [the pipes] off." When Vladimir received this information, he raised his eyes to heaven and vowed that if this hope was realized, he would be baptized. He gave orders straightway to dig down above the pipes, and the water supply was thus cut off. The inhabitants of Kherson were accordingly overcome by thirst and surrendered.

Vladimir and his [troops] entered the city. ... He sent messages to the Emperors Basil and Constantine in the capital, Constantinople [modern-day Istanbul], saying:

> **"Behold, I have captured your glorious city Kherson. I have also heard that you have an unwedded sister. Unless you give her to me to wife, I shall deal with your own city [Constantinople] as I have with Kherson."**

When the emperors heard this message, they were troubled, and replied:

> **"It is not [right] for a Christian to ... marry a pagan. If you are baptized, you shall have her to wife, inherit the kingdom of God, and be our companion in the faith. Unless you do so, however, we cannot give you our sister in marriage."**

Continued on next page

Two Stories about Conversion, Continued

Vladimir's Conversion, Continued

When Vladimir learned their response, he directed the envoys of the emperors to … tell them … that he was willing to accept baptism. When the emperors heard this report, they rejoiced, and persuaded their sister Anna to consent to the match. … Vladimir desired that the princess should herself bring priests to baptize him. The emperors complied with his request and sent forth their sister, accompanied by some dignitaries and priests. Anna, however, departed with reluctance "It is as if I were setting out into captivity," she lamented; "Better were it for me to die here."

But her brothers protested:

> **"Through you, God turns the Russian land to repentance, and you will relieve Byzantium [Greece] from the danger of grievous war. Do you not see how much evil the Russians have already brought upon … Kherson? If you do not set out, they may bring on us the same misfortunes."**

… The princess [finally] embarked on a ship and … set forth from Constantinople across the sea and arrived at Kherson. …

Prince Vladimir was suffering, at that moment, from a disease of the eyes and could see nothing. He was in great pain. The princess [told him] that if he [wanted to be cured] of this disease, he should be baptized with all speed; otherwise, it could not be cured. When Vladimir heard her message, he said: "If this proves true, then surely the God of the Christians is great," and gave order that he should be baptized.

The Bishop of Kherson, together with the princess' priests baptized Vladimir. As the bishop laid his hand on [the prince], he [got back] his sight. Upon experiencing this miraculous cure, Vladimir glorified God, saying: "I have now perceived the one true God." When his followers beheld this miracle, many of them were also baptized.

Vladimir was baptized in the Church of St. Basil, which stands in Kherson on the square in the center of the city. … The palace of Vladimir stands beside this church to this day, and the palace of the princess is behind the altar. After his baptism, Vladimir took the princess in marriage.

Adapted from: *The Christianisation of Russia* (988). at http://www.dur.ac.uk/a.k.harrington/christin.html and from *Medieval Russia's Epics, Chronicles, and Tales* edited by Serge A. Zenkovsky. New York: Penguin Group, 1963.

Look at Vladimir's Conversion

Mini-exercise   Do the study tables. Follow the directions in each table.

The people of Kherson were allies of the _____

(Circle only **the letter** that applies.)

a.	the Roman Catholics and the German princes.
b.	the emperor in Constantinople and the Byzantine Greeks.
c.	the Russian princes of Moscow and Kiev.
d.	The Bulgarian khans and their vassals.

What did the emissaries emphasize about the Greek Orthodox religion?

(Write you answer below.)

If the emperors of Byzantium had <u>not</u> agreed to marry their sister to Prince Vladimir, what would Vladimir probably have done?

(Circle **all the letters** that apply.)

a.	Vladimir probably would have married someone else.
b.	He would have taken his troops and sailed home.
c.	Vladimir would probably have sent troops to conquer Constantinople.
d.	Vladimir would probably have given up converting to Orthodoxy.

Continued on next page

291

Look at Vladimir's Conversion, Continued

Matching	
Draw a line from the people in **Column A** to the religion they belonged to, in **Column B**.	
Column A **People**	**Column B** **Religion**
People of Kherson	They were Roman Catholics, led by the Pope.
People of Constantinople	They were mostly Greek Orthodox.
Russian people	These people were probably Orthodox.
Germans	They were Muslims and worshipped Allah.
Bulgars	These people were pagans at the time of this story.

Compare and contrast the two conversions

What to do   You are going to compare and contrast the Khazar conversion of Khan Bulent with the Slavic conversion of Prince Vladimir.

There are lots of similarities and many differences between the two stories. Before you start writing, read **Tips** on the next page, which will give you a good idea of how to use the graphic organizer to help you organizer your thoughts:

➤ Read the **Tips for Compare** first.

➤ Then complete the graphic organizer for comparing the two conversions.

➤ Next read the **Tips for Contrasting**.

➤ Then do the graphic organizer for contrasting the two conversions.

Continued on next page

Compare and contrast the two conversions, Continued

Tips for Comparing

Below is the **Compare** part of an organizer. Do you recognize it? You last used this organizer with the two Kari's.

Compare
Write about how
the two conversions are alike or similar.

1.	Both Khan Bulent and Prince Vladimir were the chief rulers of their people.
2.	
3.	
4.	
5.	
6.	
7.	
8.	
9.	
10.	
11.	
12.	

Continued on next page

Compare and contrast the two conversions, Continued

Contrast

Attribute or Trait	Khazar Conversion	Russian Conversion

Tips for Contrast

➤ Before we explain the **Contrast** section of this organizer, let's review a little about attributes or traits (They are the same for any organizer.)

➤ Attributes or traits are especially important when you contrast two things or try to figure out what makes two items different.

➤ Notice the first column under **Contrast**: It says **Attribute or Trait.**

Look at the next section: It gives details and examples of attributes and traits.

Key Point

When you contrast any items, you must make sure that you find differences about the same trait or characteristic.

Let's look at a couple of examples, which follow.

Good Example

You are looking at two baseball bats. You like the colors of the first – blue and black -- better than the colors of the second – yellow and green.

You have a valid contrast because you are contrasting the bats on the same axis or trait or attribute: **COLOR**.

Continued on next page

Compare and contrast the two conversions, Continued

Importance of Attribute/Trait

A difference has to come from something that is common to the two items you are contrasting. If the contrast is not based on a common attribute or trait, it is not a valid contrast and will make no sense.

As you can see, you have to figure out the attribute or trait that is common to the things you are contrasting. This axis, attribute or trait:

- Is the baseline for your contrast.
- Guides you in what to look for in order to contrast the two items.
- Is a general feature of the two items.
- Helps you sort the details of the items so that you can find the contrasts.

Think of a maple tree and a rose bush. List all the different attributes or traits or characteristics you can <u>contrast</u> a maple tree with a rose bush, to show how different they are. We have started you with the first one.

(Write the traits below.)

i.	The **size** (a trait) of a maple tree and a rose bush are different.
ii.	
iii.	
iv.	
v.	
vi.	

Contrast the two conversions

How to do it

➤ List the traits in the column marked **Attribute or Trait**.
➤ Then check which conversion is an example of the trait.

> **You can only mark one box for each trait. For example, if the Khazar conversion is an example of the trait; the Russian conversion cannot be an example of the same trait and vice versa.**

We have started the table with a couple of examples.

Contrast for Khazar and Russian Conversions

Attribute or Trait	Khazar Conversion	*Russian Conversion*
One version includes a dream	X	
One version has a war		*X*
This version includes a marriage.		*X*

Continued on next page

Summarize your comparison and contrast

Writing

Now, write a comparison and contrast of the two conversions. Look at **Tips** below to help you in your writing.

Tips

> ➢ First write a short paragraph about the two conversions, just briefly describing them. Don't make any contrasts or comparison.

> ➢ Then write about the similarities, that is, all that is common or alike to both the Khazar and the Russian conversions. These are what you wrote in the **Compare** table. (Do **not** mix any items from **Contrast** in this part of your writing.)

Next write about the differences.

> ➢ Use the items that you wrote under **Trait or Attribute** in **Contrast** as part of your topic sentences.

> ➢ For example: The trait might be: "different ways of finding out about religions." Your topic sentence might read: **"Bulent and Vladimir used different methods to investigate various religions."**

> ➢ Then you would support **the topic sentence above**, about the different methods, with specific details from each story.

What is *interfaith*?

Where religions meet

You have seen where religions meet:

- Alexander the Great and Simon – the conqueror and the conquered.
- The Khazar and the Russian conversions: Seeking a better way to believe.

Now read one more story. Keep in mind:

- The ways the two sides viewed each other.
- The manner in which they interacted with each other.
- How they treated each other.

St. Francis meets Sultan Malik al-Kamil

St. Francis di Bernadone, born in 1182 in northern Italy, is popularly known and loved as the poor, generous, traveling friar who talked with birds, tamed wild beasts and sang the "Canticle of Creation." But Francis was once also an ... emissary of peace and nonviolence.

Francis lived in the political turmoil of the 13th Century when ... [Western Roman Catholicism] fought ... crusades against the Muslims. ... During the fifth crusade, in 1219, Francis began an amazing journey that directly opposed the attitude that produced the crusades. In response to the Christian-led crusades to restore Jerusalem and the Holy Land to Christianity, the sultan had decreed that anyone who brought him the head of a Christian should be rewarded with a Byzantine gold piece.

Francis began his resistance to the crusades by meeting first with his own religious leaders, begging Cardinal Pelagius, the Christian commander, to stop the fighting. Pelagius refused. Francis then took a companion, Brother Illuminatus, and set out, unarmed, to visit Sultan Malik-al-Kamil, the nephew of Saladin, leader of all Muslims. The men of the sultan's army captured Francis and Illuminatus and dragged them, beaten and exhausted, to the sultan, just as Francis had wished.

The sultan was receptive to these two unarmed messengers from the enemy camp. St. Bonaventure, in his life of St. Francis, described the event,

> **"The sultan asked them by whom and why and in what capacity they had been sent, and how they got there; but Francis replied that they had been sent by God, not by men, to show him and his subjects the way of salvation and proclaim the truth of the Gospel message. When the sultan saw St. Francis' enthusiasm and courage, he listened willingly and pressed Sr. Francis to stay with him."**

Francis' enthusiastic desire to share the Gospel with the sultan, without insulting Islam or refuting Mohammed, was unique. In their encounter, both St. Francis and the sultan changed. When Francis finally left to return to Italy, the sultan showered him with many gifts and treasures. Because he had no interest in worldly wealth, Francis refused all the gifts, except one: an ivory horn used by the muezzin to call Muslims to prayer from the minaret [tower] on the mosque. On his return to Italy, Francis used it to call people for prayer ... .

Continued on next page

What is *interfaith*?, Continued

 Francis also shared, [with his community back home in Italy,] his new and deep respect for his Muslim brothers and sisters, breaking … the cycle of enmity [hate] and misunderstanding that fueled the crusades. Francis was especially struck by the Islamic five-times daily prayer and the practice of prostrations [bending down] in worship of Allah; his letters urged Christians to adopt a similar practice: To make prayer a part of everyday life, in effect to remember God in everything you do.

After his encounter with Francis, the sultan placed Francis under his personal security and provided Illuminatus and him with safe-conduct through Muslim states. From then on, several accounts relate that he treated Christian prisoners of war with unprecedented kindness and generosity.

Meeting the sultan confirmed for Francis that we are all brothers and sisters. Neither man converted the other, but they met each other as men of God. Their meeting appears to have changed more than Francis and the sultan. Almost immediately we see some art work in the eastern world showing these two men. One of the sultan's own spiritual counselors (a Sufi) supposedly had engraved on his tomb that the meeting between a Christian monk and the sultan changed his own life.

> Adapted from: http://darvish.wordpress.com/2008/12/23/st-francis-meets-sultan-malik-al-kamil/ and from: Galen K. Johnson. *St. Francis and the Sultan: An Historical and Critical Reassessment*. At: http://www.emu.edu/cjp/spi/readings/PAX-559-reading-1-Johnson-on-Francis-and-Sultan.pdf.

Define *interfaith*

What to do

You are going to write your own definition of interfaith.   Include:

> ➢ The character and attitude of people in an interfaith meeting.

> ➢ The kinds of "r"eligious experiences that define interfaith.

You can use any of the selections in this text, but must also include some of the other texts in this chapter.

Be sure to read **Tips** before you use the graphics organizer that follows to help you organize your thoughts about interfaith.

Continued on next page

Define *interfaith*, Continued

Tips

Tips

> ➤ Look at the **Interfaith Organizer** below as you read about it.

> ➤ Select five texts to use in the table. Be sure they are interfaith stories.

> ➤ Under **Important Interfaith Trait/Attributes in the Tale** write what you think are the important characteristics of an interfaith meeting. Get these traits from the five stories you have selected. We have filled in a couple for you.

> ➤ List the characters from the five stories you have selected.

> ➤ Then check off those interfaith traits that the characters you listed show. Remember, to check the last three boxes (your own traits) for Francis and Sultan Malik and for Alexander the Great and Simon, if necessary.

Interfaith Organizer

Characters	Important Interfaith Traits/Attributes in the Tale				
	Respect	Tolerance			
Francis and Sultan Malik	X	X			
Alexander the Great and Simon	X				

Continued on next page

Define *interfaith,* Continued

Writing

Based on your completed **Interfaith Organizer**, write your own definition of interfaith. Read **Tips** below to help you write.

Tips

➤ The main subjects of your writing will probably be the traits that you came up with in the organizer. Each of them should be part of a topic sentence.

➤ Details to support the topic sentences should be examples of the interaction, attitudes, opinions, etc. of any of the persons showing the trait in the table.

Pairing is important

Since interfaith is two-way, you need to show how each side showed a trait in your example. For example, if you are writing about respect as a trait of interfaith, you might write about Alexander the Great and Simon this way:

"Alexander, who was a pagan, showed respect for Judaism by saying that God dwelt in the Hebrew temple that he visited with Simon. Simon showed his respect for Alexander by saying that Hebrews boys that year could be named "Alexander" in honor of the conqueror."

Pairing like this is very important. It shows the give-and-take of both sides in an interfaith situation.

Using pairing, a **paragraph** might look like this:

Topic sentence about interfaith trait, followed by:

- **First Example: One pair from the same story, followed by:**

- **Second Example: Another pair from a different story, followed by:**

- **Possibly a third pair from another story, which is followed by:**

- **Paragraph closure or final sentence(s).**

For your notes

SOURCES

Printed Sources

Bleech, Linda Ward. *Context Clues and Figurative Language* (Grades 4-8). New York City: Scholastic, 2006.

Ibid,. *Short Reading Passages & Graphic Organizers to Build Comprehension.* New York: Scholastic, Inc., 2001.

Costa, Arthur L. and Rosemarie M. Liebmann (Editors). *Supporting the Spirit of Learning: When Process is Content.* Thousand Oaks: Corwin Press, Inc., 1997.

Ennis, Robert H. *Critical Thinking.* Upper Saddle River: Prentice Hall, 1996.

Forms and Elements of Literature (Middle/Upper Grades) St. Louis: McDonald Publishing Company, 1998

Lancelot-Harrington, Katherine. *America Past and Present: Volume III.* New York City: Newbury House Publishers, 1985.

Reading (Grade 5). Columbus: School Specialty Publishing, 2006.

Schwartz, Robert J. and Sandra Parks. *Infusing the Teaching of Critical Thinking and Creative Thinking into Elementary Instruction.* Pacific Grove: Critical Thinking Press and Software, 1994.

Summerfield, Geoffrey and Judith Summerfield. *Reading(s).* New York City: Random House, 1989.

Writing Practice (Grade 4). New York City: Scholastic, Inc., 2003.

Electronic Sources

NOTE: Besides the electronic sources in the text of this volume, some useful sites for critical thinking and for various literary genres are listed below.

http://www.americanpoems.com/. Collection of American poetry.

http://www.bartleby.com/113/. Excellent site for American authors and examples of their poetry.

http://www.bookrags.com/ebooks/5403/. Good commentaries on various American writings.

http://childrens-stories.edigg.com/. Collection of fables, short stories, myths for children.

http://www.coping.org/write/percept/assumps.htm. Good site on critical thinking resources.

http://www.dowlingcentral.com/MrsD/area/literature/Terms/Metaphor.html. Excellent information, particularly for high school, on studying literature.

http://www.earlyamerica.com/earlyamerica/milestones/commonsense/text.html. Information about early American writers like Tom Paine.

http://www.edhelper.com/language/facts_and_opinions.htm. Good site for helping students to distinguish between fact and opinion.

http://www.edhelper.com/language/Reading_Skills.htm. Good reading skills and comprehension exercises for middle schoolers.

http://www.edhelper.com/language/Similes_and_Metaphors.htm. Explanation and exercises on similes and metaphors.

http://www.graphic.org/links.html. Excellent site with free graphic organizers.

http://www.historyforkids.org/learn/greeks/religion/myths/daedalus.htm. Good source of history and history-related topics such as myths.

Continued on next page

Electronic Sources, Continued

http://www.gutenberg.org/wiki/Main_Page. Best site for free world wide literary text to download - can't be beaten.

http://www.huntel.net/rsweetland/literature/instruction/assessment/outcmsStrylmnsGras.html. Site shows student requirements for literature by skill level.

http://www.literacymatters.org/content/text/cause.htm. Good site for cause and effect.

http://www.peterpappas.com/journals/greatdebates.htm. A good source for the lesson on debates. Excellent text examples. Site is excellent for advanced students.

http://www.readwritethink.org/lessons/lesson_view.asp?id=907. Good examples of similes in poetry.

http://www.loudlit.org/. Site has poetry and prose that is appropriate for reading out loud with students.

http://ncseonline.org/NAE/bibliographyResults.cfm?find=seattle. Excellent site on Native Americans and ecology.

http://www.pitt.edu/~dash/type0333.html. Site has all the versions of Little Red Riding Hood.

http://www.poemsaplenty.com/poems/category/index.php?id=39&poemcategory=DinosaurPoems. Examples of dinosaur poems.

http://www.poets.org/viewmedia.php/prmMID/16116. Excellent site for poems.

http://www.refdesk.com/books.html. Excellent source of definitions and examples of various technical, education, and literary terms.

http://www.short-stories.co.uk/. Good collection of short stories.

http://www.teachervision.fen.com/graphic-organizers/printable/6293.html. Another good site of downloadable graphics organizers.

Continued on next page

Electronic Sources, Continued

http://www.uncp.edu/home/canada/work/allam/general/glossary.htm. One of the best glossaries of literary terminology.

http://www.uncp.edu/home/canada/work/canam/whitman.htm. Good commentary on Walt Whitman; includes his life and career.

http://www.virtualsalt.com/crebook4.htm. Good site with lots of information about assumptions and inference.

http://en.wikipedia.org/wiki/. A general online encyclopaedia which is free.

www.ingramcontent.com/pod-product-compliance
Lightning Source LLC
Chambersburg PA
CBHW081323310526

45789CB00018B/2275